STOCKTON

SUNRISE PORT ON THE SAN JOAQUIN

To Dad & Mom

Best Wishes

Olana Davis

STOCKTON IN 1858

BIRDS EYE VIEW OF THE CITY
STOCKTON
SAN JOAQUIN COUNTY 1870 CALIFORNIA

STOCKTON

SUNRISE PORT ON THE SAN JOAQUIN

BY OLIVE DAVIS

PICTORIAL RESEARCH BY SYLVIA SUN MINNICK

AMERICAN HISTORICAL PRESS
SUN VALLEY, CALIFORNIA

DEDICATED TO
MY GRANDCHILDREN,
KNOWING THE PAST GIVES UNDERSTANDING
OF THE PRESENT, SO YOU CAN PLAN THE BEST
POSSIBLE FUTURE.

PHOTOTOGRAPH CREDIT CORRECTIONS

FROM	TO
Stockton Development Center	California State Archive
Stockton Public Library	Cesar Chavez Central Library
Steve Periera	Steve Periera Photography
Genna Kennedy	Courtesy Yvonne Brown, Collection of Genna Kennedy

Library of Congress Catalogue Card Number: 98-74146

ISBN: 1-892724-00-6

Bibliography: p. 162
Includes Index

CONTENTS

Frontispiece
The expansive and develop-
ing nature of the inland port
is shown here in this 1870s
view of Stockton, originally
rendered by Augustus Koch.
Courtesy, Amon Carter
Museum

INTRODUCTION

Stockton is a modern commercial center influenced by both land and water. The land is the rich soil of the delta and the Great Valley of California, which makes it the center of the most diversified agricultural area in the world. The water is provided by the mighty San Joaquin River and the California Delta, which links Stockton to San Francisco Bay and the sea.

This book is written for the general public to encourage a better understanding of this unique place. Stockton has always been a supply base, even for the California native before the appearance of the white man. It became a transportation hub for riverboats and pack animals during the Gold Rush. Later railroads and modern highways reversed the flow of supplies toward instead of *from* the outside world.

Stockton has been a city populated by those who recognized needs and were inventive enough to serve those needs. Captain Charles M. Weber, the city founder, was a man of vision ahead of his time. There have been conflicts, for Stockton has often been a city without strong leadership, a place where everyone had a voice. It is a cosmopolitan city, accepting large influxes of people who were absorbed yet remain identifiable, adding to the rich social fabric.

It has been a city heavily influenced by world events. Yet in turn it has had a strong influence on the outside world. Farm machinery developed locally helped change world agriculture. The birth of the tank shortened World War I, and during World War II Stockton became "the supply base of the Pacific."

The port that greeted the '49ers now docks ships that carry the products of the Great Valley to distant lands. In recent years the delta waterways have turned into a recreational paradise. Now modern homes use the abundance of water to enhance everyday life. Stockton is a pleasant place in which to live, with a mild climate and rich soil. It is a productive city and a place of opportunity, for it is also a growing city.

History tells of what went before but it can also help one to understand the present. This book will have served its purpose if it does this in a small way.

Olive Davis
Stockton, California

ACKNOWLEDGMENTS

This book would not have been possible without the assistance of many institutions and individuals. At the head of the list in providing references and graphic material is the Stockton Public Library, under Director Ursula Meyers and her staff, especially librarian Isabel Benson, in the reference department. The California Room Collection in the library is outstanding for local research. The Holt-Atherton Pacific Center for Western Studies, under Dr. John Bloom, and the San Joaquin County Museum, under Director Michael Bennett and assistant Debbie Mastel, also contributed with both reference and graphic material.

Reference material was provided by the California State Library California Collection, the State Law Library, and the San Joaquin County Library. The Stockton Community Development Department proved to be an excellent resource. Individual collections of resource and graphic material filled the gap where other material was not available. These included materials from Estella Magnuson, Carol Grunsky, Lillian B. Steel, Delmar McCombs, Jr., and the San Joaquin Delta History Class, Glen Kennedy, and Tillio Boggiano. A special thanks goes to Bonnie Davis who acted as a reader and kept the author on track, and to Dr. James Shebl who read the final manuscript for historical content. Others who gave support and assistance were D. David Smith, Dean DeCarli, Ilka Hartmann, Stuart Gibbons, Gunter Konold, Gerald Sperry, Elizabeth Davis, and Jean Cain.

Those institutions and persons who assisted with illustrations alone were equally important to the finished book. These include: the Amon Carter Museum in Fort Worth, Texas; the Bancroft Library in Berkeley, California; the Haggin Pioneer Museum in Stockton, California; and the Stockton Development Center under Neal Starr.

Private collections provided many of the previously unpublished illustrations in this volume. These include the collections of Mrs. John Kennedy Cahill, Mary Ann Lawrence, Glenn A. Kennedy, Betty Galli, Richard S. Minnick, Sr., Mel Bennett, Mrs. Victor Stamper, Tom Shephard, and Dr. Maynard Lang.

I.

TRAPPERS, TRADERS, AND SETTLERS

A farmer toiling in his field looks up and sees the superstructure of an ocean vessel as it steams far from the sea on the placid San Joaquin River. The river turns southward but the ship heads into the channel toward the sunrise. It travels the route of thousands of '49ers who rushed to the promised land for California gold. The ocean-going ship reaches port at a city 70 nautical miles east of the Golden Gate. Commuters, caught up in the early morning rush, pass unnoticing as the old vessel nudges a dock at the busy port. A seagull dives into the churning wake of a tug, catching tasty morsels for a gourmet meal. Soon the ship's holds are gaping wide to receive golden grain, the bounty of the land.

The sun rising from the snow-covered Sierra Nevada range silhouettes a modern city. It is a commercial center in the heart of the Great Valley, with a population in excess of 220,000. To the north, east, and south lie fertile plains blanketed with intensive farming—orchards, vineyards, and row crops—and contented cattle in green pastures. To the west is the river delta with almost 1,000 miles of waterways and some of the most fertile farming land in the world. Nicknamed Tuleburg but officially named Stockton before the Gold Rush, Stockton became the first American-named city in California. The unique setting alone confirms the city's slogan, "Stockton, Someplace Special."

The land around Stockton has always been influenced by the sea. Long ago when early life forms were still evolving, the foundations of the Sierra Nevada and the Klamath ranges were formed, while the rest of northern California was covered by a shallow sea.

Approximately 60 million years ago an east-to-west fault line occurred north of present-day Stockton. The fracture caused the rising of a parallel ridge, forming a peninsula which projected into the sea as far west as the present Diablo range. Other parts of the emerging lands of central and northern California were reclaimed by the sea, but not the Stockton Arch. It had risen from the depths to stay.

The Sierra Nevada range rose to newer and greater heights as the Great Valley trough dropped lower on both sides of the Stockton Arch. During the California Ice Age, which started about 3 million years ago, virtually all the Sierra Nevada Mountains above 3,000 feet were covered by sheets of ice. These glaciers ground the mountains away, and, as the ice melted, the rivers carried the alluvial sediment down to fill the Great Valley trough, in some places by as much as 200 feet.

As geologic forces raised the north and south ends of the Great Valley, the San Joaquin and Sacramento rivers took the runoff waters to the sea via the Carquinez Strait and San Francisco Bay. Where the rivers met they came under the influence of the Pacific tides that flowed in through the strait. This slowed the flow of both rivers and a huge delta marsh developed in the valley west and northwest of the future Stockton site.

Like all delta land, the San Joaquin-Sacramento Delta was rich in all the materials necessary to support lush vegetation. Both birds and animals, the descendants of ice-age survivors, flourished as the delta teemed with life.

This engraving of Charles M. Weber captures Stockton's founder at the height of his influence, benevolence, and prosperity. His generosity in providing for broad avenues and numerous parks are reminders of the many legacies Weber left to the people of Stockton. Courtesy, Stockton Public Library

A *stone mortar, tongs, and gathering baskets were essential to every Indian household for food preparation. These* *instruments were found locally during excavation for county roads and house construction. Courtesy, San Joaquin County Historical Museum*

Archeological data puts man in the delta region by 2,400 B.C. The people of the Early Horizon period—the first known people of central California—were hunters and food gatherers. Experts believe that these people were of the Hoken language stock (one of several basic languages identified with early California man), and were later succeeded, in about 1,000 B.C., by those of the Penutian language group. This change may have come about by conflict, for some skeletal remains from this time period have been found with stone weapons embedded in their bones.

The people of the new Penutian language stock first occupied only the delta and San Francisco Bay areas, but later expanded into the Great Valley until they controlled both the Sacramento and San Joaquin river lands. Eventually, the original Penutian stock divided into many separate tribes and distinct language groups. Three of these groups lived in or near the delta—the Yokuts in the south, the Miwoks in the central and eastern part of the delta, and the Wintons in the north, near present-day Sacramento. By the time Eric the Red sailed the Atlantic more than 1,000 years ago, an Indian culture was being defined in a place that would someday be known as Stockton.

There is some question as to which tribe was the

last to occupy the Stockton site before the appearance of the Spaniards. It is likely that at various times either Yokut or Miwok language groups lived near the sloughs at the head of the Stockton Channel. It is known that the native population—estimated at about 150,000 in the Great Valley alone—was large for an aboriginal people. The land was capable of supporting more people than in most untilled areas of the world—approximately two per square mile—not high by today's standards but very high for hunters and food gatherers who did little to manage their food resources.

Was there an Indian village on the site of the city? Yes, there are indications of at least two or three in the immediate vicinity. Carl Grunsky, who was born in Stockton in 1855, noted in his reminiscences the exact location of a round "Indian Hole," a bowl-like depression about three feet deep, southwest of Sutter and Church streets near Mormon Slough. This was no doubt the floor of a "temescal," or sweathouse, in what was probably a fishing village. Grunsky understood the main village to be north of the Stockton Channel west of Banner Island.

An imaginary visit to an Indian village on Mormon Slough would take us first to the center of village life, the sweathouse, located downstream from the main village so that bathing could take place below the area where drinking water was secured. Family dwellings consisted of a cluster of tule huts constructed of tule mats tied to willow frames. Acorn cribs, built on stilts with woven twigs and brush to allow free air circulation, prevented drying acorns—a staple food—from molding. The visitor would probably see village women pounding acorns into meal in stone or oak mortars.

The observer would notice that the Indians did not put their houses under the giant valley oaks, for although this location would seem logical, the Indians knew that on a hot summer day an oak tree could drop a limb without warning, crushing anything beneath it. Instead they used the great trees to hang strips of meat and fish to dry, out of reach of marauding coyotes and bears. Often the women sat under a shelter of tule mats set on willow poles, working on baskets or deerskins, their full tule skirts gracefully fanned out on the ground. In winter the women wore deerskin and cloaks of skins or feathers. The tattoo marks on their chins were beauty marks much desired by young girls, just as young boys desired the status of admittance to the sweathouse.

On a typical day, most of the men who were not out hunting could be found in the sweathouse working on tools, preparing for a hunt, or simply socializing. The sweathouse was covered with earth, except for a hole in the roof to vent the smoke from the firepit inside. The keeper of the sweathouse started the fire early in the morning, for that was his only occupation; since others provided him with food, he did not need to fish or hunt. As the temperature rose inside the house, the men began to sweat profusely, using the curved rib-bones of deer to scrape and clean the skin. Finally, the men ran from the sweathouse to jump into the waterhole to bathe, then returned to stand in the smoke and rub sweet-smelling herbs on their skin to eliminate all human scent. Painting the fronts of their bodies white to resemble the bellies of their game, and taking their deer or elk disguises, the men would go out to hunt. This method was so apt to fool the game that occasionally a hunter could get close enough to touch an animal.

When the hunter returned with his kill, he divided up the meat among the people he felt obligated to feed. Superstition prevented him from eating his kill, so he waited to feast on a neighbor's gift of meat. His spouse would work the hide into leather for clothing, such as the deerskin apron he wore. Feather headdresses were sometimes worn, picket-fence style, around the head or at other times like a topknot, perhaps mimicking the valley quail. It is apparent that these people were highly aware of their environment. Even their dances imitated the animals they held in reverence.

The tribe's only form of food management was done with fire. In fall they set fire to the grasslands and marshes, preventing the brush and tule reeds from taking over the land and providing tender new shoots to entice the game, particularly the area's vast herds of tule elk.

Food was abundant in the delta area: rabbits and quail inhabited the grasslands and were snared with hair loops; Mormon Slough yielded freshwater clams by the basketful; fish were caught in weirs, basket traps, or nets; waterfowl were enticed with decoys. The women gathered seeds and dug roots, never leaving the village without their digging sticks. In season, there were wild grapes and berries to be gathered. It was a way of life suited to the environment that supported it—and the Indians found riches in the land that not only sustained life but allowed a culture to develop.

Were these tribes of the Yokut or Miwok language group? It suffices here to say that experts cannot agree. But recent studies indicate that the Yachicumne, Chilamne, and Pasasime tribes who inhabited the lands adjacent to or south of the Calaveras River, were Yokuts. Those on the

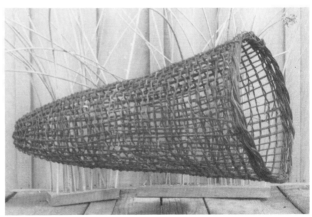

Top: A duck-shaped decoy hidden among the tule lured waterfowl to the Indians' readied nets, providing food for the tribe. Courtesy, San Joaquin County Historical Museum

Above: Indians caught fish in weirs, basket traps, or nets. This wicker fish trap was used in the smaller streams of Northern California. Courtesy, San Joaquin County Historical Museum

Mokelumne River—the Mekelkos, Lalas, and Machacos, were Miwoks. As to the villages located in the Stockton area, the best evidence indicates the natives were probably of the Yachicumne tribe, members of the Yokut linguistic group.

The Yokut tribes were, as a rule, peaceful. They were somewhat short in stature and had a tendency to be plump. Although the last chief of the Yachicumne, Mauresto, was described as a big and powerful man, one anthropologist has described the Yokuts as generally being "round people with no sharp angles."

Early historians agree that the Indians in the delta were envied by other tribes for their great abundance of food. It took strong people to hold the territory, and this abundance apparently made them physically stronger than less fortunate tribes. The Miwoks, who inhabited the Mokelumne River bottomlands, were tall in stature, many of them over six feet in height. Other tribes regarded them as "bad" Indians because

Miwok and Yokut tribes found abundant fish, game, and waterfowl in the tule marshes. Wild fruit and seeds supplemented their diet, as well as the tule plant's roots, pollen, and seed. The tule plant stalks provided fiber for clothing and shelter. Courtesy, San Joaquin County Historical Museum

of their aggressive tendencies. It has been reported that they considered themselves the elite of the California Indians.

Each tribe had a main chief, or headman, as well as a war chief. Thus, the main chief of a warring tribe could negotiate from a neutral position when it came time to make peace. There is no doubt that the Yokuts and Miwoks living in close proximity to each other had occasional work for their war chiefs.

In 1772 the first Spanish explorers looked to the lands of the Yokuts and Miwoks from the Diablo range. Four years later an expedition, led by Jose Joaquin Moraga from the newly founded San

Francisco Presidio, made an attempt to explore the edge of the delta.

In the beginning, the Spanish padres had gone alone into the Great Valley to bring back Indian converts for their missions. In 1811 Padre Narcisco Duran recorded his adventures on a trip into the delta by boat. He visited an Indian village near the present French Camp and traveled back downriver. He wrote:

We had traveled but a short distance when we found waiting for us one hundred and thirteen natives, part Yachicumne and part Mokelumne, half of them painted and armed with an aspect of war. At 6 o'clock we took leave of them giving them wheat, etc. and they promised us that they would come visit us at the mission.

This must have come to pass, for mission records show 118 Yachicumnes and 143 Mokelumnes were converted at Mission San Jose following this date. It is known that many Indians tended to go voluntarily to be converted when bad weather affected their normal food supply. It seemed though, that when they became less hungry, they became more homesick and left the missions. Christianized Indians were sent out to bring back runaway Indian "converts" to the missions, which created continuous turmoil among the Indians of the valley.

In the ten years following Duran's 1811 visit to the valley, the Indians on the east side of the San Joaquin River became more and more resistant to Spanish control. There were many forays into the valley by the Spanish who continued to try to punish runaway Indians. In spite of this, more Indians returned to their native haunts. It eventually became clear that the Spanish controlled the west side of the San Joaquin River while the east side belonged to the natives. This is not surprising, in view of the fact that the Spanish empire had been crumbling for some time and proved to be too weak to prevent the Russians from establishing a fort north of San Francisco. The Mexican government gained independence, and in 1822 California officials recognized a Mexican government independent from Spain.

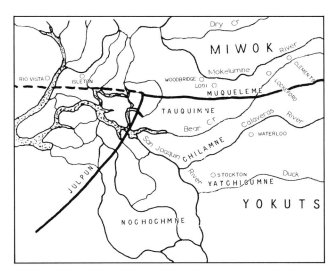

This modified map details the approximate boundaries of the Central Valley Miwok and Yokut Indians. Delineating the locations of the modern towns onto this Indian territorial sketch overwhelmingly suggests that the Yokut Indians were the primary group in and around the Stockton area. Courtesy, Carl Zucker

Where the Spanish had restricted trade, the new Mexican government encouraged trade with foreign ships. Monterey was named the official port of entry into California. Heavy import and export taxes were levied to help pay for the provincial government. Increased shipping brought more foreigners, who often married local California residents. The missions thrived in this era and welcomed visitors, but the understaffed military authorities became uncomfortable and suspicious of foreigners. This was the situation in Mexican California in 1826 when a party of American fur trappers, under the leadership of Jedediah Strong Smith, literally sneaked in the back door of California.

In the spring of 1827 Jedediah Smith and his party of trappers arrived in central California. While Smith and two of his men set out to cross the Sierra Nevada range to return to the annual trappers' rendezvous in the Rockies, most of the party spent the remainder of the year in a base camp on the Stanislaus, southeast of future Stockton. No doubt they trapped along the

American fur trappers and members of the Hudson's Bay Company made an annual trip to the French Camp area to set up summer beaver trapping headquarters. A beaver pelt is shown here stretched on a willow frame. Courtesy, San Joaquin County Historical Museum

Seemingly tranquil, the French Camp Slough area teemed with activity in the 1820s and 1830s. American explorers and French fur trappers used the French Camp area in the summer months for their headquarters due to the abundance of elk, bear, and beaver. Courtesy, San Joaquin County Historical Museum

lower delta and nearby rivers, for they reported taking a considerable number of furs out of the area, including the Calaveras and Mokelumne rivers, in January 1828.

The stories Smith's party told of trapping in California opened the gates to future ventures. The Hudson's Bay Company, already feeling the pressure of American trappers in the Western mountains, sent Alex McLeod south to trap in California. He traveled as far south as the Stockton site, and camped on a small lake—present-day McLeod Lake in the heart of Stockton. The location became a regular rendezvous for trappers who traveled by canoe in the lower delta.

McLeod's expedition was followed by a continual stream of trapping parties in the valley, all reporting numerous brushes with the Indians. The trappers were a tough breed of men, who sometimes made

friends with the local Indians, but who just as often destroyed them, whichever suited their ends. One French trapper, Michel la Frambois, was an exception, for he employed a peculiar brand of frontier diplomacy. An American officer wrote of him, "He had traveled in all parts of the country and says he has a wife of high rank in every tribe, by which means he has insured his safety." (There is, however, no record of his taking a local wife.) French Camp on the southern edge of present-day Stockton was named for la Frambois, who camped there in 1832 and many summers thereafter.

The only written record left by a trapper who came to the Stockton area is the diary of John Work, leader of a Hudson's Bay party of 100 men, women, and children who left Fort Vancouver on August 17,

1832. Within 11 days Work wrote of an illness that plagued his people. It was a recurring fever that struck almost everyone in his party and caused some deaths before the trip was over. The party proceeded into California to camp at Sutter Buttes where they met la Frambois in January of 1833. The illness subsided somewhat during the winter but returned to plague the group as soon as warmer weather and mosquitos returned. No doubt this was the unidentified illness that devastated the interior California Indian population that year. This could have been malaria transmitted by mosquitos, for Work complained of the hordes of these insects that kept everyone from sleeping at night, and in his diary he noted every cooling ocean breeze through Carquinez Strait that brought relief from the heat and insects.

On July 9, 1833 Work set up camp on "a small creek or bay" near McLeod's Lake, perhaps on Stockton Slough. Three days later he sent all the canoes out into the delta for a 12-day trip. On Saturday the 13th he wrote an account of a skirmish with the local Indians. Some natives visited the camp while others tried to steal the trappers' horses. A

battle followed and Work recorded the event in his diary:

Two [Indians] were killed and others wounded, but they concealed themselves among the rushes and could not be found. One of them bent his bow to fire an arrow at me behind my back but one of the women attacked him with an axe and he fled with the others.

They were attacked again in the night and Work reported, "Arrows were falling thick among us." The party broke camp the next morning and continued south. On July 24 the entire party, those on land and those in canoes, convened again at McLeod Lake. Work recorded their take from the vicinity as 45 beavers and 14 otters. He also noted that two canoes which had been in the lake were gone, presumably stolen by the Indians.

Work led his party north the next day. Work himself was so ill by the time he arrived back at head quarters that he did not go out hunting for some time. But it was the Indian population, which had little resistance to the alien disease, that suffered the most that summer. The American trapper, J.J. Warner, later reported that he found the valley depopulated in the summer of 1833, saying he saw no more than six or eight Indians from the head of the Sacramento to the "great bend of the San Joaquin." The trapper reported seeing skulls and bodies under every shade tree. He also found the remnants of a funeral pyre at a village site near the Stockton area. This was the first of a series of epidemics (fevers, smallpox, and other communicable illnesses) that would continue to kill the native population in the Great Valley.

During the next three years the California authorities seemed satisfied to leave the interior valleys to the resources of Michel la Frambois, who spent each winter trapping from French Camp. John Marsh, an American, arrived on the scene in 1836. He was looking for a cattle ranch and had been enticed by Jose Noriega to look at his land grant at the eastern base of Mount Diablo, west of present-day Stockton. Marsh wanted to see the rest of the country first, so he and Noriega joined an exploring party. The group came to a dry stream at dusk, crossed it,

He had selected the location after consulting with the Hudson's Bay authorities in Vancouver. The Mexican California authorities gave their permission for the settlement, thinking that Sutter would make a good barrier in the northern interior between the Mexicans and those who coveted their territory, namely the Americans, British, and Russians. Sutter, they believed, might also act as a control on the Indians.

In the meantime Marsh's letters to Missouri had begun to take effect. On May 9, 1841, the Bartleson-Bidwell party set out overland for California with Marsh's invitation in hand. A smaller group caught up with them on May 23. One of these late arrivals was a 27-year-old man who would become the founding father of the city of Stockton before the decade ended. He was Charles M. Weber, a German immigrant, born February 17, 1814 in Steinwenden, Germany. Christened Carl David Weber (he changed his middle name to "Maria," perhaps to better blend with the California population), he was the first child of Henrietta and Carl Gottfried Weber, the town's minister.

The Weber family moved to Homburg, where the father became the minister and president of the Reformed Local Church Council. Young Weber received instruction at the Royal Bavarian Preparatory School. Seldom near the top of his class, he did continue his education toward the university until a proclamation was issued that all students in public schools must declare loyalty to the king of Bavaria and the Catholic Church. His education apparently continued under private tutoring. In 1836 Weber left for America, accompanied by a cousin, Theodore Englemann. The two separated upon landing in New Orleans. Englemann went to Illinois to visit his uncle while Weber remained and went into the business of "traffic and merchandise," according to an early local history.

Within the next two years Weber came down with yellow fever, recovered and went to Texas, returned to New Orleans, and became ill again. A doctor advised him to seek a cooler climate, so he headed north. He was apparently going to his uncle's but got sidetracked in St. Louis only 25 miles from his destination. He must have read Marsh's letters and

and set up camp on the north bank. Early the next morning they were surprised to find themselves in the midst of an area covered with human skulls and bones. They called the river Calaveras, the Spanish word for skulls. Two previous reports of these skulls had been made but the name Calaveras did not appear on maps until after this encounter.

Marsh was determined to make California part of the United States. He bought Noriega's grant and occupied it in the spring of 1838. Marsh began to write letters to Missouri telling of the virtues of California and inviting settlers to come to his ranch.

In 1839 John Sutter, a Swiss fortune hunter, arrived in California with the intentions of establishing a settlement in the Sacramento Valley.

learned of the Bartleson-Bidwell party. He also met at least one of Sutter's acquaintances, for he secured a letter of introduction to Sutter. He joined the small group that managed to catch up with the main party heading west.

The old trapper, Thomas Fitzpatrick, guided the party as far as Soda Springs in Idaho where the group divided. More than 30 men (including Weber), one woman, and a little girl set out for California across unknown territory, following a map drawn by Marsh, who had never traveled the route. They made it across the desert and into California over the Sierra Nevada mountains through the Emigrant Basin area of present Tuolumne County. They traveled down the ridge between the Stanislaus and the Tuolumne rivers into the Great Valley in late October of 1841.

The emigrants doubted their location until an Indian told them they were just two days' distance from John Marsh's ranch. They were disappointed in the land they found in California, but were told there had been a drought, the worst in years. There had been no rain for 18 months. They hurried to the ranch, where Marsh treated them to a feast. Their host was pleased with his success in getting them to California and he was generous in his welcome. Some of the party went on to San Jose, but Weber and Henry Huber, another German, set out for Sutter's

Facing page: Swiss fortune hunter John A. Sutter arrived in California in 1839, planning to establish a settlement in the Sacramento Valley. From Cirker, Dictionary of American Portraits, Dover, 1967

Above left: Charles Maria Weber's permit to travel to North America was issued in the Rhine District of the Royal Bavarian Government in 1836. The passport included a description of the 22-year-old Weber. He was 5'10", had black hair, black eyebrows, brown eyes, a healthy complexion, and no distinguishing marks. Courtesy, The Bancroft Library, University of California, Berkeley

Above: When the Bartleson-Bidwell Party began their overland trip to California in 1841, Nancy Kelsey, wife of Benjamin Kelsey, was the only woman accompanying the group of 31 men. Although the Kelseys did not remain in the Stockton area, Nancy Kelsey continued her friendship with Helen Murphy Weber well into the 1870s. Courtesy, Pacific Center for Western Historical Studies, University of the Pacific

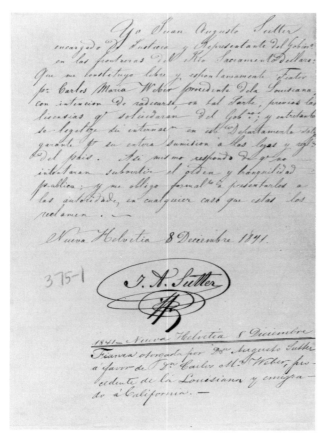

John A. Sutter of Sacramento
wrote a character reference for
Charles M. Weber in 1841.
Weber worked as Sutter's
overseer in the winter of 1841
and intended to settle in
California. As his sponsor-
executor, Sutter assured
General Mariano Vallejo that

Weber "would not subvert the
public order and tranquility,"
guaranteeing Weber's complete
submission to the laws and
regulations of the country.
Courtesy, The Bancroft
Library, University of
California, Berkeley

Fort. On the way Weber first saw the site of his future
city, Stockton.

When they arrived at the settlement Sutter
immediately hired Weber as an overseer. The rains
finally came, and the small settlement bloomed the
following spring. Weber grew flowers, vegetables, and
tobacco plants from seeds Sutter had never gotten
around to planting. Weber first met Jose Jesus, chief
of the Siakumnes (the Stanislaus River tribe), at the
fort during the winter.

By the following May, Weber was ready to move
on, so Sutter gave him a passport to San Jose. If

Weber took the regular trail between the fort and San
Jose, he would have once again passed the Stockton-
French Camp area. Certainly he saw a different sight
than he had during the dry season, for now the grass
was green, flowers were blooming, and the oak trees
were in leaf. No doubt the game had returned to feed
on the succulent clover and new grass that had
sprouted after the long drought.

Ilka Hartmann, in her book *The Youth of Charles
M. Weber*, describes the feelings of the young man so
far from home:

*Charles Weber was struck by the beauty of San Joaquin
County and loved the oak-studded and tule-covered land.
It was like home to him. Weber had no difficulty in
realizing that the valleys of the San Joaquin and
Sacramento Rivers could become a paradise of fruits and
flowers. Similar work to that necessary here had been done
in Lanstuhl Swamps during his youth.*

Charles Weber soon made friends in San Jose and
formed a partnership with William (generally known
as "Guillermo") Gulnac, a naturalized Californian
who had originally come from New York state. The
two men established a store, a blacksmith shop, and a
flour mill. They manufactured sea biscuits, which
were much in demand for the many ships that docked
on the coast. They also began the first manufacturing
of shoes on the West Coast, and Weber established
an inn, the Weber House.

In the spring of 1843 Gulnac, in the company of
Peter Lasson, drove some cattle to the valley. Lasson
later said, "Gulnac wanted to stop at French Camp
and offered me part of the land. I do not know if he
had a grant."

Since the Indians were unruly, Gulnac did not stay
either, and both went north together. Indeed, Gulnac
did not have a grant, for Sutter issued the first
recorded document on June 8, 1843, stating that the
land in which Gulnac was interested was unoccupied
and available for settlement. On July 14, Gulnac filed
an application with the California governor for
11 square leagues on the east side of the San Joaquin
River. Six days later Weber bought Gulnac's interest
in the San Jose businesses and immediately left for

Sutter's Fort. He sent word out to arrange a meeting between himself and José Jesus, the Siakumne chief. The two met, and Weber laid out his plans. He appealed to Jesus' hatred of the California authorities by telling him the Americans wanted to settle in his area out of reach of the Spaniards in case trouble arose between the United States and Mexico. Weber indicated he believed, as did the chief, that this area was not within the California territory. Perhaps Weber also assumed that his future settlement would be the western frontier of the United States.

The Indian chief suggested Weber settle in the Stockton and Mormon Slough area. This was an astute move on his part, for the settlement would give his tribe additional protection from the Mokelumne tribe. The two men made a pact to support and protect each other, which they both kept.

In order for Weber to own land in California he had to become a Mexican citizen, so as soon as he returned to San Jose he requested naturalization. Soon after, Gulnac resubmitted his grant application. This time it contained the Sutter document issued the previous June. Governor Manuel Micheltorena questioned the large size of the grant application, and wanted to know who else would be included in the settlement. On January 4, 1844, Micheltorena agreed that Weber could be granted citizenship. Nine days following this action, Micheltorena issued a grant to Guillermo Gulnac for "his benefit, his family and eleven other families." It included 11 square leagues on the east side of the San Joaquin River from the river to the "laguna called that of McCloud" [sic]. The grant was titled Campo de los Franceses on the original document.

Weber received his Mexican citizenship from the governor on February 20, 1844, and became eligible to own land. It is obvious that Weber's actions, which coincided with Gulnac's efforts to acquire land, had some relationship.

James Williams, a young settler, went to look at the Gulnacs' grant and made arrangements with Gulnac "to go on the land." He visited the site in late July, and a month later he returned in the company of James Lindsey. They brought 100 head of horses and cows to stock the land and several Indian vaqueros to

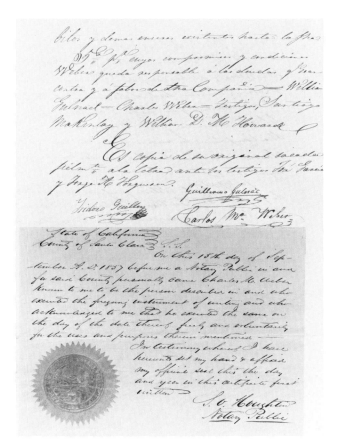

Guillermo (William) Gulnac and Charles M. Weber formed a commercial partnership in San Jose that ended a year later in 1843. A dispute over the legal ownership of the El Rancho de Campo de los Franceses, a 48,747-square-acre land grant, caused Weber to produce this partnership dissolution document in court, showing the signatures of Gulnac, Weber, and their witnesses. Courtesy, The Bancroft Library, University of California, Berkeley

care for them.

Two tule huts were built, one for Lindsey on the present site of Stockton City Hall and a second 300 feet to the north for Williams. Within a short time, other settlers, one of them David Kelsey, arrived on the scene. Kelsey and his family had migrated to California from Oregon during the summer and they were looking for a place to settle down. Kelsey moved his wife and children into a crude tule house at French Camp, which was included in the grant.

In the meantime, Californians had launched a

rebellion against the Mexican-appointed Governor Micheltorena and his convict troops, who raided the countryside whenever they received no pay. While Micheltorena marched north against the retreating forces of the rebel leader, General José Castro, Weber and other San Jose merchants, concerned about being raided by the Mexican troops, organized volunteers to defend San Jose. They managed to keep the governor at bay and even got him to sign a treaty agreeing to send most of his objectionable soldiers back to Mexico.

While Castro waited for Micheltorena to do as promised, Sutter decided to enter the conflict. He was no doubt motivated by his desire to obtain certain land grants confirmed by the governor. In December Weber went to Sutter's Fort to dissuade him from getting involved in the affair. Weber was captured by a "Council of War" supporting Micheltorena and headed by Sutter. Weber was ordered to be put in chains, but was apparently left free on his honor at Sutter's settlement. It was here that he met his future wife, Helen Murphy. She was a member of the Steven-Murphy emigrant party, which barely escaped the fate of the later Donner party in crossing the Sierra Nevada mountains.

Sutter marched out of his fort to fight beside Micheltorena on New Year's Day, 1845. He was eventually captured by Castro, who succeeded in driving Micheltorena and his troops out of California. After the conflict was over Castro made Weber a "captain" of his "Auxiliary Forces of Infantry." Weber must have cherished the title, for he used it for the rest of his life, even though he never actually fought for the Mexican rebels.

While the conflict was going on a tragic episode unfolded at the Stockton settlement. In early winter the Kelseys ran out of food and went to San Jose for supplies. Before leaving San Jose, Kelsey visited "a sick Indian." Almost as soon as he, his wife, and young daughter returned to French Camp he too became ill. His wife gathered up some of their belongings, put her small daughter and ailing husband in their wagon, and headed for Sutter's Fort for help. When they reached Lindsey's hut on McLeod Lake he convinced them to stay overnight, assuring Mrs.

Commodore Robert F. Stockton, an American naval officer, forced the last Mexican troops out of California. Impressed with Stockton, who had rescued him from Mexican captivity, Captain Charles M. Weber named his city after the young officer. Courtesy, Stockton Chamber of Commerce

Kelsey that Williams could minister to her husband. The next morning, however, the illness had advanced to reveal its dreaded identity. It was smallpox. As soon as Lindsey, Williams, and the others in camp realized this, they hastened to leave. Thousands of Indians in the valley had died from the disease and even Sutter had threatened to shoot any man who entered his fort with the illness.

Soon Mrs. Kelsey became ill and lost her sight. Eleven-year old America Kelsey was left alone to take care of both her parents. Her father died three weeks from the day he was stricken. Fortunately, a group of herders came upon the scene. They hesitated at first, but finally George Wayman helped the little girl bury her father. He also waited until Mrs. Kelsey and America, who had by now contracted the disease, recovered enough to travel to San Jose. America Kelsey later became the bride of George Wayman, the kind young man who had come to her aid.

Lindsey and Williams returned to camp two weeks after the Kelseys left. While Lindsey stayed alone in camp to tend the stock as Williams went off to Sutter's Fort for supplies, a tribe of Indians from the Amador area in the mountains to the east raided the camp, driving off the livestock and burning the house. A group of men riding back to Sutter's Fort found Lindsey's arrow-pierced body floating in McLeod Lake. Thus the land grant was again unoccupied and showed little prospect for settlement with the double dangers of smallpox and hostile Indians.

Early in April 1845 Weber, now a Mexican citizen, bought Gulnac's interest in the land grant. The document reads in part, "he [Gulnac] sells to the aforementioned Don Carlos Maria Weber for the sum of two hundred dollars, half in silver and the other half in goods, which are to be paid to the said vender at the time of the act of sale."

Later Bennet B. Nell, a friend of Gulnac's, remarked that Gulnac told him he sold to Weber "because the time in which he [Gulnac] was to settle the grant had nearly run out and he could not do anything toward it in time." Nell further said "there were only 40 to 45 days left to settle the land."

Weber planned for early settlement of the valley, for William Buzzell, son-in-law of David Kelsey, would later testify in Weber's claim before the U.S. Land Commission, "I was at Captain Weber's place [San Jose] in the spring of 1845, when he was collecting and purchasing cattle to put on the place." (All Mexican land grants, including Weber's, had to be presented to the U.S. Land Commission after California became part of the United States. Weber's claim was confirmed in 1854.)

Probably because of the threat of smallpox and hostile Indians, Weber did not visit his newly acquired grant. He did, however, by the end of the year, purchase another grant in the San Felipe Valley, perhaps to maintain the cattle he was collecting for

the Stockton grant.

Weber was fortunate that the California Department of Assembly confirmed and made official the grant title to El Rancho del Campo de los Franceses on June 15, 1846. It was just nine days later, on June 24, that the Bear Flag was raised over Sonoma, beginning the open American civilian rebellion against Mexican rule in California. Many of the Americans involved in the Bear Flag Rebellion would later settle in or near Stockton.

Weber refused General Castro's orders to organize a California unit against the Bear Flaggers and became the prisoner of war of his former friend. Castro imprisoned Weber at San Jose in 1846, and he was not released until the American Navy officer, Commodore Robert F. Stockton, forced the last Mexican forces out of California. Weber was one of the rebellion's minor characters, thrust upon occasion into a major role. He has been designated everything from a hero to a villain in the affair. One must suspect he was somewhere in between. After his release Weber did accept an order from Commodore Stockton to organize a group of volunteers to defend San Jose again, this time from California ranchero owners. Weber alone was blamed by the Californians for the raids on their ranches, when horses and cattle were taken, supposedly to provide for the needs of American troops.

Weber received orders and counter-orders from the U.S. military authorities. Finally, after he was ordered to give the horses back to the Californians, which he did, he was told to retrieve them again for his volunteer forces. In disgust, he answered, "Excuse me, if you please, I have done everything to the Californians. Let other people do the balance." These words have been taken as a confession by some historians, but one might wonder if it was sarcasm. Was he perhaps saying that since he had been blamed for all the wrongdoings he felt that others should take the blame for what followed? Nowhere is there any indication that Weber made excuses for his actions or answered his critics. He was not a man of words but a man of action. His energy and perseverance led to the founding of a vigorous new city on a major slough of the San Joaquin.

I.R.A.PARKER. 4. BAKERY & HOTEL, BY STREET MURPHY & WHITEHOUSE, WHERE NOW
STANDS THE INDEPENDENT OFFICE.   5. GOVERNOR EDWARDS.

STOCKTON IN 1849 .
FACSIMILE OF A PAINTING NOW IN POSSESSION OF THE SAN JOAQUIN COUNTY PIONEERS.

I. WEBER'S STORE.   2. TREE, WHERE N.E.COR. DEPOT NOW STANDS.
6. STORE SHIP.   7. PRISON SHIP.

II.

A TOWN OF "PROMISING IMPORTANCE"

By 1847 the war with Mexico was over and California was secured under the military protection of the United States. At last Charles M. Weber turned toward settling his land grant in the Great Valley. He drove a large herd of stock onto the land in August of 1847 after the river had receded enough to allow cattle to cross. James McGee and three vaqueros stayed to tend the stock and Andy Baker was hired as a hunter. The men built a tule house on the peninsula between Stockton Slough and McLeod Lake in the area now known as Weber's Point. Oak logs were cut and a fence was built across the land between the slough and the lake. A wide ditch was dug, providing a moat around the camp.

Next Weber had a village site surveyed by Walter Herron. A full block of town lots was set out in an area now bounded by Weber Avenue, Center, Main, and Commerce streets. Early historians reported he named the village Tuleburg, but there is testimony to the contrary. Daniel Murphy, in a deposition for Weber's land grant case, said, "I first heard the name [Stockton] in the fall of 1846." There is also an entry in John Sutter's diary of October 14, 1847 referring to two Indian boys who "brought a passport from Weber in Stockton."

In September Weber enticed a large wagon train from the East to stop and look over his land. He offered free land if they would stay. While camped on Weber's Point a member of the party, Ruth Gann, presented her husband, Nicholas, with a fine son, William; it was the first recorded birth in what is now San Joaquin County. Seven or eight families remained in Stockton, but the others went on to San Jose.

Those who stayed on the grant lived in tents and built tule and brushwood huts close together on the new townsite.

Weber went to his store in San Jose and soon returned with a launch-load of supplies for those who agreed to stay. William Buzzell, David Kelsey's son-in-law, brought his family and built a log cabin in the newly surveyed town.

Caleb Herriman was hired by Weber to construct more tule houses on the land. Soon others arrived, including P.B. Thompson, John Sirey, George Fraezher, Harry F. Fanning, and Eli Randell, the latter to clerk in Weber's store. A corral was constructed on the north side of the Calaveras River, extending the settlement's boundaries.

News of the settlement began to spread. On November 6, 1847 the *California Star*, a San Francisco newspaper, reported that near Lindsey's Lake (McLeod Lake) "a town is building of promising importance."

On January 24, 1848, an event occured that gave further impetus to the development of the town. Sutter's employee, James Marshall, discovered gold in the millrace at Coloma. He immediately went to tell Sutter the news, and although both tried to keep the discovery a secret, by mid-February the word was out at Sutter's settlement.

Weber and his settlers immediately organized the Stockton Mining Company. The stockholders, besides Weber, were Joseph Buzzell, Andrew Baker, Thomas Pyle, George Fraezher, Dr. J. Isabel, and John M. Murphy of San Jose. Most of the Stockton Mining Company men set out for the hills with supplies from

W.H. Creasey painted Stockton in the days of the '49ers, creating a sense of the bustle and activity present within the young inland port town. From History of San Joaquin County, California, *Thompson and West, 1879*

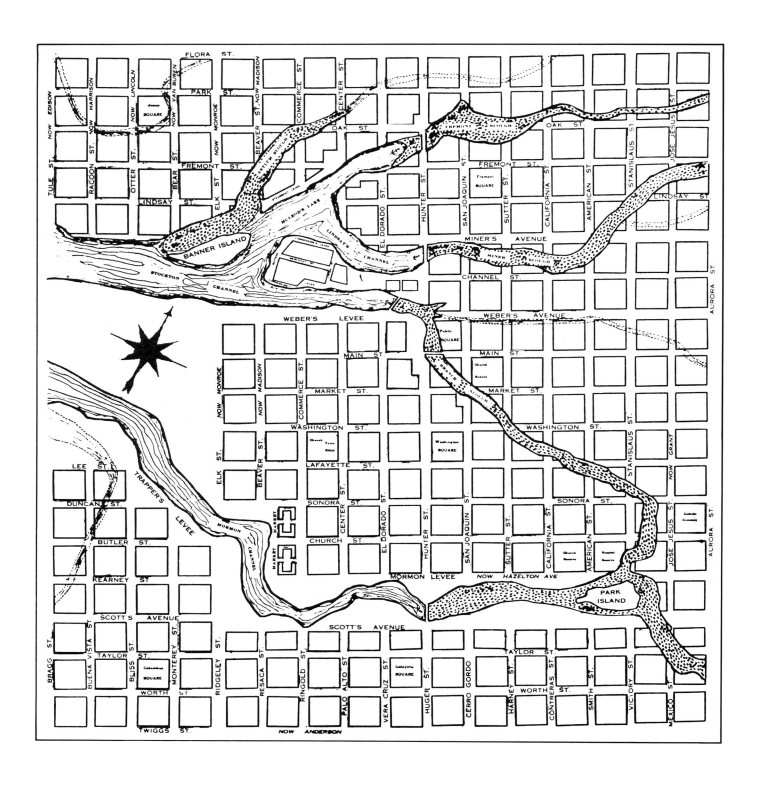

Weber's store and 25 head of cattle, leaving the settlement to the care of herders. Weber went to San Francisco for additional supplies, including trinkets and items that would appeal to the Indians. He took his merchandise by boat to Sutter's embarcadero and by pack train to the hills.

Weber's partners first prospected and found some gold on the Mokelumne but soon moved on to the north. There they met Weber and set up a store on a small creek below what is now Placerville. The settlement was soon referred to as Weberville. The partners sold supplies at a great profit, prospecting only in their spare time.

By June the population of northern California had been smitten with gold fever. Soldiers began to desert their posts, and sailors their ships. California's military governor, Col. Richard B. Mason, decided to visit the mines to get some firsthand information. He stopped at the Stockton Mining Company store in Weberville on July 7 and secured a fine gold specimen from Weber, which he sent to Washington with his official report.

As the rush for gold gained momentum, Weber sent a message to his friend, Chief Jesus, asking for 25 able-bodied men to learn the techniques of finding gold. The Indians arrived and proved adept at the task. They were soon trading gold for goods and trinkets. Weber sent them back to their home grounds to look for the precious metal and instructed them to report their findings to his overseer in Stockton. Soon word got back to Weber that coarse gold had been found on both the Stanislaus and the Tuolumne rivers.

The Stockton Mining Company men and others moved to the newly discovered southern mines. One of the Indians brought in a kidney-shaped nugget weighing 80.5 ounces. The Stockton Mining Company received $3,000 for the specimen from the

company of Cross and Hobson of San Francisco, and the remarkable piece was sent on to the Bank of London to show the richness of the gold strike in California. So it was that gold from the Stockton Mining Company, which was sent to the capitals of the United States and England, fired the starting gun for a worldwide race to California.

On September 1, 1848, Weber withdrew from the Stockton Mining Company, receiving a settlement of $6,347. While others rushed to the new goldfields, Weber returned to his fledgling town. He went to San Francisco and purchased a small two-masted sloop, which he named *Maria*, filled it with supplies, and sent it back to Stockton.

Weber bought lumber and had it shipped to Stockton. He planned to build a store on the peninsula, on the north side of Stockton Channel, but the lumber was unloaded on the south side by mistake. Because of the difficulty of transferring the material to the intended location, Weber had the building erected near the intersection of what is now Weber Avenue and Commerce streets.

Weber continued to offer town lots to anyone who would build on them but still had few takers, for most preferred to dig for gold. He had, however, set his course and continued to deal in commerce. He purchased the brig *Emil*, with its load of supplies, in San Francisco and sailed it to Stockton, where he tied it up on the levee and for a time used it as a store.

Walter Colton of Monterey, who had founded the first newspaper in California in 1846, wrote about Weber while visiting Stockton in November 1848:

Charles Weber, a gentleman much esteemed for his liberality and enterprise, is the owner of the land now occupied by the town, and many leagues adjacent. He has given spacious lots to all who would erect buildings. His policy is marked with wisdom; he will find his advantage in the results. His ample store is well filled with provisions, groceries and ready made clothing. The amount of business is immense and the profits would phrensy our Philadelphia merchants.

Other Stockton Mining Company men went into business in the new town. Murphy and Ferguson

This close-up of the one square mile of Stockton surveyed by Major Richard P. Hammond features Stockton Channel, Banner Island, and Mormon, Branch, Asylum, Miner, and *Fremont sloughs. In later years many of the north-south streets were changed to reflect continuity. Courtesy, Stockton Public Library*

opened a bakery in a tent at the corner of Levee and Hunter streets. Sirey and Whitehouse opened an "eating house" a block to the east on the levee.

Weber's store, the first lumber building in town, was completed in January 1848. (Before, there had been only brush or tule huts or tents, and the log house of Joseph Buzzell.) George Belt and Nelson Taylor soon set up competition in a tent store immediately east of Weber's business. The company of Lane, Douglas, and Rainey also opened a general store, and Jim Davis built a house on the levee and opened a saloon.

Weber must have decided that his original survey was inadequate for a town growing so rapidly, for he hired Major Richard P. Hammond to do another. The town lots were laid out a mile square with the east-west streets parallel to Stockton Slough. Charles Weber was a man of vision. He planned well with wide avenues leading to the boat landing. He also set aside 17 blocks of the city for public lands and parks. The survey was completed in June of 1849—none too soon, as the Gold Rush was gaining momentum.

Stockton became the gateway to the southern mines, located between the Mokelumne and Merced rivers. Every boat from San Francisco came loaded with passengers. Once in Stockton, there were only two ways to get to the goldfields—by foot or by

The Matteson & Williamson plant, shown here in the 1830s, was founded by Donald C. Matteson and stood on the corner of Main and California streets. Matteson, a local blacksmith, manufactured plows, reapers, harvesters, and other farming equipment in 1852.

Williamson joined Matteson's company in 1865. Other early businesses in this same area included the Stockton Iron Works, beginning in 1868, and the Commercial Hotel, which began in 1875. Courtesy, Stockton Chamber of Commerce

horseback. Baggage became as expensive to move as people, costing an average of 30 cents a pound to haul from Stockton to the hills. Needs were recognized, for more new businesses were set up to accommodate the travelers. A livery stable was built by William Fairchild and operated by the Owens brothers. Grayson and Stephens, a San Francisco firm, opened a wholesale liquor store. One of their best customers was Little Jack Keller who ran the Shades Saloon. Two partners, Thompson and White, opened a general store in a tule hut. Isaac Zachariah and his brother set up a clothing store in a six-by-ten-foot tent; starting with an inventory of $50, they made over $20,000 in six months. A 100-foot-square gambling tent contained 20 tables that were busy all the time.

During the heady days of the Gold Rush,

thousands came through Stockton seeking gold. One of the first steamers to arrive in the Sunrise Port came in September of 1849. It was a small side-wheel steamer, the *Captain Sutter*. The boat arrived unexpectedly, with flags and streamers flying. The townspeople went wild, gathering on the levee and raising cheer after cheer. The steamboat commenced daily runs on the river and gave the town its first frequent and regular communication with the outside world.

As Stockton became established as a supply base for the southern mines, many of the miners looked for easier ways to find their fortunes. Stockton was full of these men, who either opened supply stores or ran pack mules to the goldfields. Many of those who had been farmers in the East saw the rich soil around Stockton and settled on the land. The first crops grown included grain and hay to feed the hundreds of horses and mules that made up the pack trains. By February 1851 *Stockton Times* editor John White estimated there were 600 persons engaged in farming within a ten-mile radius of Stockton.

During the fall of 1849, at the height of the frenetic Gold Rush activity, Bayard Taylor, a *New York Times* correspondent on the way to the gold-fields, described what he saw as he rode into Stockton:

A view of Stockton was something to be remembered. There in the heart of California, where last winter stood a solitary ranch in the midst of tule marshes, I found a canvas town of a thousand inhabitants and a port of twenty-five vessels at anchor. The mingled noises of labor around—the click of hammers and the grating of saws, the shouts of mule drivers, the jingling of spurs, the jar and jostle of wares in the tents, almost cheated me into the belief that it was some commercial mart—familiar with such sounds for years past. Four months only had sufficed to make the place what it was and in that time a wholesale firm established here (one of a dozen) had done business to the amount of $100,000.

When Taylor returned to Stockton on his way back from the goldfields, he witnessed local justice. Three drunken men had attempted to molest a woman. A complaint was made to Alcalde George G. Belt, and two of the men were found. They were "seized, the witness examined, a jury summoned and the verdict given without delay." The punishment was 50 lashes for one and 20 for the other, plus 48 hours to get out of town on threat of death. The men were stripped to their waists and tied to a tree. Taylor was appalled at the behavior of the crowd, who "jeered, laughed and accompanied every blow with coarse and unfeeling remarks." Those who professed to be against such punishment told him they knew no other recourse but death. Death was the sentence of two others convicted of murder a short time later. The law was local, swift, and very much in the hands of the people or sometimes the mob.

The Stockton business community became anxious to have a formal government, so Alcalde George Belt, in his official capacity as judge, ordered an election to select officers for the city. The election was held and nine men were elected to serve. But the election was declared illegal by the first county judge, Benjamin Williams, who was elected under the direction of the newly organized California legislature. Judge Williams decided Alcalde George Belt did not have the authority to call a city election. The court further ruled that the aldermen elected to serve were personally responsible for all debts incurred by the city while they were in office. This was a damaging

The side-wheeler Sagamore *made frequent trips into the Stockton harbor during its short 11-month service before its engine room exploded. This picture shows Stockton's waterfront where the* El Dorado, *the* Captain Sutter, *the* Roberson, *the* Mariposa, *and many other vessels competed for the Stockton trade during the town's early years. Courtesy, Stockton Chamber of Commerce*

start for the city, making the men a laughingstock for the rougher elements in town. It also discouraged many a prudent man from seeking office in the future.

Christmas Day, 1849 marked an unhappy occasion for the city, as one entire block containing much of the business district lay smoldering in ruin. On Christmas Eve a fire had destroyed the tent and brush shelters within the area bounded by Main, Center, Levee, and Commerce streets. The townspeople had tried desperately to douse the fire with a bucket brigade from the slough, but approximately $200,000 worth of hard-to-replace merchandise had been destroyed.

Shortly after this disaster San Francisco's business district also experienced a devastating fire. The merchants there demanded money owed them from the distressed Stockton businesses, which forced

many of them to close their doors. Recovery became a top priority in the town, and by February the business community joined together in petitioning Weber to remove his store-ship from the harbor and to use his influence to get others to do the same. They stated that the blocking of the harbor by idle ships impaired the development of the city. Weber responded, and most of the ships not actively used for transportation were moved to Mormon Slough. Once again supplies began to flow into Stockton in preparation for the opening of the roads to the mines.

On March 16, 1850 the town's first newspaper, the *Stockton Times,* was published by co-owners and editors Dr. Henry H. Radcliffe and John White. The paper announced the opening of the Stockton House, a hotel built by Jacob Bonsell, John Doak, and a man known to historians only by his surname, Scott. The establishment was located on El Dorado Street on the peninsula side of the channel. The first theatrical performance, put on by a travelling company organized in San Francisco, was soon held in the new hotel. A variety of recitations and acts were offered and were proclaimed a great success.

On March 15, 1850 a group of men met in George Belt's general store to discuss forming another town council. The *Times* reported immediate protests.

Some of the townspeople professed they could not afford more government, as it would mean "money out of everyone's pockets." But the newspaper supported the move, citing the prevention of crime as the town's number one priority, and noting the need to eliminate the custom of the carrying of deadly weapons by almost every man in town. The *Times* editor, John White, further suggested a prison chain gang be used to clean the streets, work on the levee, and do other badly needed tasks about town. Although the city had no facilities for enforcing the law or retaining prisoners, the county government leased the brig *Susanna* for a jail. Prisoners were shackled below deck, and parts of the ship not needed for the jail were used as storage or for the sale of merchandise.

The business community continued to thrive, and in the spring of 1850 it was reported that $30,000 worth of business a day was being transacted. "Between two and three thousand persons arrived in Stockton last week," the *Times* reported on one spring day. Yet another setback was in the making, for notices were published of the Foreign Miners' Tax passed by the state legislature. Licenses to mine were required for anyone not a citizen of the U.S. or who had not become a citizen under the Treaty Guadalupe Hidalgo, Indians excepted.

Groups of foreign miners soon left the goldfields because of the miners' tax, and mountain businesses stopped ordering merchandise from the Stockton suppliers. Stockton merchants sent a petition to the governor demanding he call the legislature into session to reduce the tax.

By 1850 committees had been organized to incorporate the city of Stockton, and had been meeting on a fairly regular basis. In June 1850 a committee recommended that a fire department be organized and officers elected. James E. Nuttman was named chief engineer, and A.C. Bradford assistant chief. One hundred volunteers enlisted to serve when needed.

The organization of the town council was finalized by San Joaquin County Judge Benjamin Williams on July 23, 1850. Judge Williams called for an election to be held at the Central Exchange (otherwise known as

Dr. George A. Shurtleff arrived in Stockton in 1849, bringing enough lumber from Chile to build the Mount Vernon House, one of the first small hotels in Stockton. Elected to the town's governing body in 1850, Shurtleff later served as mayor, county sheriff, and superintendent of the State Asylum in Stockton. Courtesy, Stockton Chamber of Commerce

the Central Exchange Saloon). The election was held on August 5 and officers were officially chosen in a non-partisan election. Samuel Purdy was elected mayor, along with seven aldermen, including Charles M. Weber, W.H. Robinson, J.W. Reins, James Warner, B.F. Whittier, Hiram Green, and George A. Shurtleff. Others elected to serve as officers of the newly organized town government were: A.C. Bradford, city clerk; G.D. Brush, city treasurer; William H. Willoughby, city marshall; E.J. Edmondson, city assessor; H.A. Crabb, city attorney; F.C. Andrew, city harbor master; and Walter Herron, city recorder.

The city of Stockon, incorporated on July 23, 1850, became a charter city of the state of California more than a month before California became a state.

III.

WEBER'S CITY ON STOCKTON SLOUGH

On October 15, 1850 the news of California's statehood reached Stockton and the townspeople rejoiced. During the next few years there would be dramatic changes in the complexion of Stockton and all of California.

Business was booming that fall as the mining towns stocked up for the winter. The city council authorized the wharf committee to supervise the building of more docks along the channel. Todd and Company announced it would cooperate with Adams Express Company. The former utilized pack animals (horses and mules) to move mail and supplies to the hills and haul gold back to Stockton; the Adams Express Company transported goods on riverboats from Stockton to San Francisco. In the year since he had first arrived one Stockton businessman, Charles Grunsky, had taken on two partners, and more business, by adding a wholesale outlet in Stockton and operating a string of pack animals that hauled freight to the hills.

Charles M. Weber, who was more concerned with building his town than with freighting to the mines, had a small two-room schoolhouse built on San Joaquin Street near Market Street. It was called the Academy, and there the town's first teacher, C.M. Blake, held class, though only for a short time. Apparently he left to seek a more lucrative occupation. The following spring the Academy was reopened under Dr. W.P. Hazelton. A group of volunteers had raised the funds and advertised "a free or public school where orderly children of proper age may receive instruction free of charge." This took place two full years before the California legislature

provided for public school funding and the city council took appropriate action to establish a city-wide school system.

Weber had also begun building a spacious home on Weber's Point. It would in a short time become a showplace among California homes. It must have been a most happy time for Weber, because on November 29, 1850 Helen Murphy became his bride in a Catholic ceremony in San Jose, six years after they had met at Sutter's Fort. It has been assumed that they did not marry sooner because of their differences in religion. Helen came from a strong Irish Catholic family and he from an equally strong German Protestant one. Charles did, however, join and remain loyal to the Catholic Church for the rest of his life. He extended his generosity to all religious denominations, donating land for every church group that asked. He also provided land for the Jewish, Catholic, and rural cemeteries as well as others.

The first recorded religious services were held in Stockton soon after the discovery of gold. On July 1, 1849 the Reverend Samuel C. Damon of the Congregational Church conducted the first Protestant service. He held it aboard a store-ship tied up on the bank of Stockton Slough. It was reported to have been the quietest Sunday ever in the town according to local historian Covert Martin.

A Catholic service was held the same year by two priests on a trip to the mines. During their stopover in Stockton they said Mass in Captain Weber's home.

A Methodist layman held a prayer meeting in a tent in the fall of 1849, and a Southern Methodist Minister, a Reverend Hopkins, dropped in on the

---

This 1867 view of Weber Avenue between Hunter and San Joaquin streets shows a pedestrian footbridge over a minor slough to the far right. The Water Syrups &

Company Building belonged to Charles Belding, who owned the Belding Soda Manufacturing Company. The Belding corner housed the Yosemite Cash Grocery Store

where the Belding Building now stands. Courtesy, Pacific Center for Western Historical Studies, University of the Pacific

Above: Competition was stiff among companies and individuals contracted to handle freight carriage from Stockton to the mines. Jasper S. Hall prepares to leave with his 12-horse team and three wagons full of supplies on the west side of Hunter Square, the center of Stockton's early business activities. Courtesy, Stockton Chamber of Commerce

Right: This Rulofson daguerreotype shows Charles M. Weber's home on Weber Point on July 4, 1856. Built in 1851, the house was purportedly one of the first permanent homes in the San Joaquin Valley, and was made of redwood, brick, and adobe. Courtesy, Pacific Center for Western Historical Studies, University of the Pacific

This photograph of Charles M. Weber's family dates from about 1858. Helen Murphy Weber posed with her son, *Charles II, daughter, Julia, and baby, Thomas. Courtesy, Stockton Public Library*

meeting and preached a short sermon.

By March of 1850 the Presbyterians were organizing a church, about the same time Methodist Elder Isaac Owen arrived from San Jose to organize a congregation. The Presbyterians completed their church building and dedicated it on May 5, 1850. The Reverend James Woods had taken a poke of gold dust collected in Stockton to San Francisco to buy the precut lumber for the structure. Charles M. Weber donated land for this church site. He also donated two lots for the first Catholic Church, erected at Washington and Hunter streets. The site was selected because many Catholics—Mexican, Spanish, Chilean, and French—lived in the immediate neighborhood.

All denominations, including the Ebenezer African

Methodist and a Jewish synagogue, soon found their place in town and Weber helped them all by giving freely of his land. The city became more civilized as the congregations grew.

Despite its burgeoning institutions, Stockton was still a frontier town. Records show that in the spring of 1851 thieves were dunked in the sloughs and flogged in the name of street justice before being rescued by the constable. The first legal execution was held under the county court system late in May. George Baker, convicted of murder, was strung up in the hanging tree, an old oak, on west Main Street. Within two weeks a horse thief was also hanged at the same spot as 500 townspeople watched. Though frontier justice prevailed, by this time the jail had been moved from the brig *Susanna* to the basement of the McNish Building.

Culture began to take root in the city with an opening performance on February 11, 1851 in the El Placer Theatre, constructed over the El Placer Saloon at the corner of El Dorado and Levee by gambler Jim Owens. *Damon and Pythias, Othello,* and *Hamlet* were all performed during one week. Seats sold for two and four dollars each; all 700 seats were sold out for the first performances.

The El Placer Saloon downstairs became the scene

This picture of an early saloon was used as an advertisement for The '49 Saloon. Partners Gustave Genecco and Paul Trucco first opened the saloon in 1905 on East Weber Avenue near the head of the Stockton Channel, but moved their facility around the corner to El Dorado Street. The business folded in 1919. Courtesy, D.W. Chan

of an important social event, a fancy-dress and masquerade ball held on February 8, 1851. The *Times* reported the dance was "filled with the youth and beauty of the place." The life of the El Placer was short-lived, however; it burned down on May 5 of the same year. Soon a second dance was held and 37 women were reported in attendance, though apparently they were not the town's social elite. One early historian makes a special note of the fact that "the first respectable dance in Stockton was held on Washington's birthday at the Stockton House." Mrs. Charles M. Weber and several of her women relatives from San Jose attended the event.

Though women added stability and social refinements to the town, they also contributed their labor. Mrs. Isaac Woods opened a girls' school in the basement of the Presbyterian church. Another early businesswoman was a Mrs. Rhodes, who operated a "fancy dry goods store" on Main Street. Zacheria's Tailor Shop hired two women to sew shirts, and there

was always a demand for cooks and washerwomen in a town where luxuries were rare and even well-to-do women did their share of work. In some cases young women were brought from Europe or the East as servants, although most soon married and set up their own households. As late as 1859 a Stockton newspaper announced, "Fifteen Yankee girls arrived Tuesday from Boston, a part of a consignment which had been previously promised. It is presumed that they will apply for positions as help, but will accept the position of wives from eligible parties." Of course, there were the prostitutes and those who served drinks in the saloons and dealt cards in the gambling

34

The first San Joaquin County Court House, located on Weber Avenue near the head of the Stockton Channel, was built on land donated by city founder Charles M. Weber. The construction of the two-story building was completed in 1854 at a total cost of $83,920. This building served as the nerve center for the local county government for 33 years until it was rebuilt in 1887. Courtesy, Stockton Chamber of Commerce

halls. One "beautiful young French woman" was reportedly brought to Stockton for the purpose of running, and perhaps lending some Continental style, to a saloon.

On March 15, 1851 the Stockton business community rejoiced as the Foreign Miners' Tax was repealed. The business community once again received orders for supplies from the hills as foreign miners returned to work. The city, which had suffered for lack of cash, soon redeemed the scrip it had issued in lieu of money and a local newspaper boasted, "Our scrip is the only paper in California that can be quoted at par."

During the spring of 1851 the volunteer firemen organized the Weber Engine Company. The volunteers met and elected officers. The city fathers agreed to purchase a hand-pulled hose cart and pump from Charles M. Weber. This was the first of many fire companies that developed into social, often political, and always competitive firefighting teams.

When, on May 3, 1851, a major fire destroyed much of San Francisco, Stockton Fire Chief James

Nuttman and other firefighters took a steamer to the city to inspect the ruins. Unfortunately, while they were gone a fire started shortly after midnight near the corner of Center and Levee streets. The hook and ladder equipment burned up before anyone could get near it, and the Weber Company pump, manned by inexperienced firemen, was nearly destroyed when it was trapped between two burning buildings. A northwest wind fanned the flames that consumed nearly six solid blocks of the city, and the Stockton firemen returned to find a major portion of their own city's business district in ruins. Undaunted, the Stockton business district immediately began to rebuild with whatever materials were available, mostly wood and canvas.

Despite the town's loss Stockton became the site of county offices, and the history of the port city became permanently interwoven with the history of San Joaquin County. The relationship between city and county officials has often been clouded with conflict. Nowhere has this been more evident than in the events involving block three, designated as "Court House Square" on the original city survey map.

The original county government was organized under the California Constitution in the spring of 1850, with a governing body of three judges known as the Court of Sessions. One of the court's first actions was to inform Weber they were ready to receive any public lands he intended to turn over to them. He responded by issuing them a gift deed of block three, to be designated Court House Square. But the judges returned it to him, requesting a more legal document. In the meantime one of these judges, Hariston Amyx, claimed squatter's rights on a corner of the square. It took considerable legal action to remove the judge and uphold Weber's claim. So it is little wonder that after the City of Stockton was finally organized in the fall of 1850, Weber deeded the square in question to the city alone. He signed the deed in August 1851, had it notarized in December, but did not have it recorded until February 1852, indicating it was not a rash action on his part.

Weber's deed to the city included all the streets, levees, and public squares, and contained a clause that this property be put only to "proper use." According

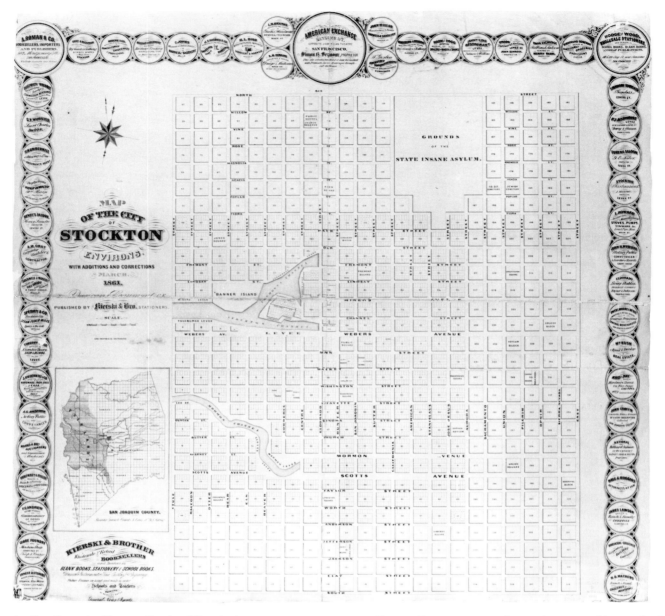

to the San Joaquin County Book of Deeds, he reserved for "himself for his own benefits, use, behalf and disposal such portions, parcel and parcels of the different sloughs, channels and bayous or creeks, contained within the limits of the city of Stockton" as marked upon the map accompanying the deed. He also reserved all rights to pass this property on to his heirs. By this single act Weber put his permanent imprint on the City of Stockton.

The state legislature, on April 30, 1851, provided for a general hospital to be located in Stockton. It was opened in a wooden structure on the northwest corner of El Dorado and Market streets, under the direction of Dr. R.K. Reid, and it soon became the practice to send all the region's mentally disturbed patients to the Stockton Hospital. In September 1852 bids were solicited for the construction of the new

Duncan Beaumont surveyed the area for this map showing the layout of the original blocks of the one square mile of Stockton. The outer blocks' parcels had not yet been delineated. Because of the inland waterway to the west, *the town could expand only to the north, east, and south. The grounds of the State Insane Asylum are clearly marked in the northeastern section of town. Courtesy, The Bancroft Library, University of California, Berkeley*

state hospital main building, which was to be erected on land donated by Weber in the northeast portion of the city. New facilities were constructed on land donated by Weber and on July 1, 1853 the hospital was dedicated as the State Asylum for the Insane. It has been operating in the same location since.

The rains never came during the winter of 1851-1852, which proved to be detrimental to mining operations. By mid-January there was a depression

Charles Grunsky spent a short sojourn digging for gold in the Mother Lode in 1849 before he settled in Stockton to become one of the town's leading pioneers. Courtesy, C.E. Grunsky, III

and a scarcity of money. One newsman noted money was not hard to borrow. "If one has good security," he wrote, "it may be obtained at 4.5 to 6 percent per month interest." Charles Grunsky wrote that his business profits had dropped from 200 percent to 25 percent during the previous year.

By the fall of 1852 Stockton was prosperous once again, but the rains started early in December and by Christmas the city was a disaster area. The Calaveras River overflowed and the streets became rivers, washing away anything not firmly fastened down. Fences and timbers riding a torrent of water battered a house off its foundation, adding to the debris that tore out two bridges downstream. Charles Grunsky, who had returned to Stockton the previous spring with his bride, Clotilde, later wrote to his family:

I had to rush out into the yard to bring in a horse, water coming up to my waist. The horse, the dog, the cat and chickens were lodged for two days in our lower story. We

lived upstairs. I felt sorry for Clotilde who had not been able to leave the house for two months.

Grunsky, like all others in town, cleaned up after the flood and got back to work as soon as possible. Grunsky's ventures are typical of those of many of Stockton's early residents, for although his business partnership soon dissolved after he returned to Stockton, he took the company farm as his share of the assets. He was doing what many others were doing, looking to the land. He was convinced the price of land was going to continue upward. He believed the land would be a good investment even if farming did not prove profitable. He did, however, continue to freight to the mines to supplement his income.

Grunsky's trips to the hills must have caused his wife considerable worry, for robberies and murders were occurring in epidemic proportions in the outlying areas. Almost every crime was blamed on the infamous Mexican bandit, Joaquin Murrieta. Anti-Mexican feelings were on the rise and one local newspaper noted the only solution was to banish the entire Mexican population from the city. Both newspapers, the San Joaquin *Republican*, which had replaced the *Times*, and the *Stockton Journal*, a Whig party paper, could be radical at times.

The Stockton Mexican population survived these troubled times, but it is little wonder that they clustered their modest homes together in an area east of San Joaquin and south of Washington streets within the sound of St. Mary's church bell. According to one early historian the populace was mostly of the peon class from Mexico. They were excellent horsemen and early in the Gold Rush had been in great demand to run the pack teams to the mines. They also worked on the sheep ranches, and were employed as vaqueros, taking care of thousands of head of cattle in the valley. A few in town manufactured and sold leather equipment for horses, and were part of the prosperous business community.

By the summer of 1852 the city had managed to recover from the devastating flood. There were reported to be 40 blacksmith and wagon shops in town. A reporter wrote, "this class of mechanics are

Safely perched on a balcony on the second floor, residents watched floodwaters rise in 1890. This scene at the corner of Hunter and Miner streets was typical in Stockton when spring runoff flooded the area. Historians and geographers noted that between 1852 and 1950 some part of the county was inundated every three or four years, but the flood during the winter of 1861-1862 proved the most widespread and severe. Courtesy, Pacific Center for Western Historical Studies, University of the Pacific

the most monied men in the county." There were two flour mills in operation. One of these was run by Sperry and Baldwin, who processed 2,000 barrels of flour during the season. A shipbuilding operation was conducted by S.H. Davis and William Emerson at Lindsey Point on McLeod Lake. These shipyards, under Davis' supervision, would launch many ships in the following years.

In April 1852 telegraph lines were completed between Stockton and San Francisco and the operators hoisted their glasses in a toast as the first message was transmitted. By spring of 1852 another new theater was completed, and it was reported there were 60 hotels and boarding houses in town, "all of them busy."

During the spring Weber offered the city the block of property at the head of Stockton Channel for a city hall. The only condition was that the city build a bridge on El Dorado Street connecting Weber's Point, the land on which his home was built, with the south bank of Stockton Slough. The city council representative replied that they had a committee working with the county judges to erect a courthouse on the square and a jail in another location. Apparently the county officials did not realize that the city alone had been deeded the square. The problem was not solved for two more years. On October 5, 1855, the city officials executed and recorded a deed giving the county "one half of the Court House Square and the improvement thereon."

In 1852 the city passed an ordinance establishing the public school system. The privately funded schools were closed, and girls and boys were placed in separate schools. The Reverend W.C. Candus took charge of the boys' school in the Academy. Mrs. Isaac Woods opened the girls' school in separate quarters on Main Street.

Though Stockton was at this point only five years old, the city was well established. It was still dependent on the miners for much of its supply business, but it was also a budding manufacturing center with farmers as well as gold-seekers to supply. As the town grew, the city fathers began to seek solutions to some of the town's problems—muddy streets, unsanitary conditions, and open gambling. Some streets were planked, and all hogs were ordered to be removed from the city's streets. The last gambling house was closed, excluding those in Chinatown, the area bounded by Bridge, El Dorado, Channel, and Hunter streets. This Chinatown had been established early in Stockton's history. In the fall of 1849 a ship resembling a Chinese junk docked in McLeod Lake; it was full of Chinese headed for the mines. Soon Chinese merchants set up shops to cater to the Oriental population. A Chinese fishing village was also established on Mormon Slough.

By mid-century the river steamboats had become an important part of life in Stockton. The city depended on the side-wheelers, and later the stern-wheelers, for the much-needed supplies that were the lifeblood of the community. Stockton newspapers took note as each new and more powerful steamer set time records on trips to and from San Francisco. As

The El Dorado Street bridge connecting Weber Point and the south bank of Stockton Slough was built at a cost of $60,000. Bob Patton, David S. Terry, and John Fisher have been identified as the three sitting on the bridge railing looking westward down the channel. The two steamers tied up to the south bank are the Amador *and the* Tulare. *Courtesy, Pacific Center for Western Historical Studies, University of the Pacific*

more boats competed, rates dropped and the business community smiled. The competition became so fierce that potential passengers heading for Stockton were sometimes literally pulled on board by overzealous crew members trying to beat the competition. In their races against time, caution was often thrown to the winds as steam boilers were pushed beyond their limits and exploded in bursts of steam and shrapnel. Passengers and crew alike were often maimed and sometimes killed by these explosions.

Stockton's newspapers railed against the dangerous conditions caused by competing steamboat companies, and the companies' owners finally decided to put an end to the problems caused by such stiff competition by organizing the California Steam Navigation Company. The change brought reliable

service, with few accidents. But ironically, the same newsmen who had criticized the companies for the accidents now took up their pens against the monopoly.

In the city's early years Stockton newspapers and Stockton politics were almost one and the same. Elections were held annually and each newspaper backed its own party's candidates. The papers were frankly biased, and heated editorializing was common. But more than once an editor was held accountable for what he wrote. When Stockton's first mayor, Samuel Purdy, ran for lieutenant governor of California, the editor of the *Stockton Journal,* John S. Robb, wrote a series of scathing articles against him. Purdy, a highly educated man of refined social graces, ignored the articles until they questioned his qualities as a gentleman. Duels had been fought over lesser offences, but Purdy decided he would not honor the editor as a gentleman. He declared he would whip Robb and teach him a lesson. He secured a whip, and a gun to back it up, and went looking for Robb. When Purdy found his man, Robb drew the gun he always carried, but Purdy was ready. Using his own gun, he hit the editor over the head, thus putting an end to the matter. The insults no longer appeared in

Stockton's Civil War veterans formed Rawlins Post Number 9 of the Grand Army of the Republic in 1868. At one time the local unit had as many as 500 members. Veterans in their eighties and nineties posed for this group portrait almost 60 years after their participation in the conflict that pitted brother against brother. Courtesy, Pacific Center for Western Historical Studies, University of the Pacific

the paper.

Editors not only attacked politicians but also each other. Two other editors, John Tabor of the *Journal* and John Mansfield of the *San Joaquin Republican*, sniped at each other constantly during one especially hostile political campaign. Tabor settled the feud by shooting and killing the unarmed Mansfield on a Stockton street. Tabor was convicted and sentenced to be hanged in the Stockton jailyard, but received a last-minute pardon from the governor.

As the issues leading to the Civil War widened the gap between North and South, many of Stockton's residents began to worry that the city's strong Southern contingent would cause conflict among the citizenry. Many Southerners had come through Stockton during the Gold Rush, for it was on the path to the goldfields for those who came by way of the Southern land route. Many were former soldiers of the recently won Mexican war in Texas. A number of these Southerners had returned to Stockton from the hills and established themselves in the city. Every newspaper in town—the *Times*, the *Journal*, the *San Joaquin Republican*, the *Daily Argus*, and the *Weekly Democrat*—had in turn carried the cause of the South as a banner. Although the city offices were all non-political, the Democratic party dominated state and national elections locally. The Southern Democrats

talked of forming a Pacific Republic if the Union was dissolved, and on several occasions flags similar to the California Bear Flag appeared in town, suggesting that California withdraw from the Union. Immediately American flags were flown in protest. The Stockton Blues, a quasi-military group of local volunteers, had both Northern and Southern sympathizers among its ranks. Although the group's primary purpose seemed to be to drill and march in parades, the Northerners in the group, fearful that the Southerners would do something rash, disbanded the unit. A new military troop, the Stockton Union Guard, was organized as a replacement, and each member was required to pledge support to the Union.

Both state and local Democrats had begun to separate into Southern and Northern camps as civil war became imminent. Despite growing factionalism, the Democrats remained in control in Stockton. When Abraham Lincoln was defeated in the 1860 presidential election in both Stockton and San Joaquin County, the Democratic editors rejoiced. They were stunned to find, several days later, that Lincoln had carried the state. Local newspapers called all Lincoln supporters "black Republicans." Having no local voice, the region's Republicans enticed the *Calaveras Independent* to move to Stockton. The new *Stockton Independent* declared that it was not attached to any party, but its editorial policy was clearly pro-Union.

As the issues polarized Stockton's citizens into two camps, old friends and business associates took up the side of either North or South. One prime example of this is the partnership of Thomas E. Ketcham and Frank Cheatham. The two had been business partners in a general store in Stockton, but before the war was over they were fighting on different sides. Cheatham

David S. Terry migrated to Stockton in the early 1850s and proceeded to bring much fame and notoriety to the town. Noted for his duel with Senator David C. Broderick, the former Texas Ranger also opened a flour mill in

Clements, was the senior partner in the law firm of Terry, Campbell, and Bennett, and served as a California Supreme Court Justice. Courtesy, Pacific Center for Western Historical Studies, University of the Pacific

owned the Hotel de Mexico located on Bridge Place where the Philadelphia House would later be built. One early historian says the place was a hotbed of secessionism, and that Cheatham was the underground leader of the Confederacy in Stockton. Cheatham eventually left California and became a brigadier general in the Confederate Army. Ketcham became captain of the Third Volunteer Regiment of the U.S. Army.

David S. Terry, the Stockton attorney whom Samuel Purdy had defeated in the first mayoral election in Stockton on August 5, 1850, had long been active in the Democratic Party. He was Southern born and Texas raised, and during the Civil War he left for Texas, where he organized Terry's Regimental Dismounted Cavalry, Confederate States of America. He was elected a colonel to lead the unit.

There was no doubt as to where Charles M. Weber stood during the Civil War. He flew the Stars and Stripes from a tall flagpole on Banner Island in McLeod Lake. More than once the secessionists replaced his banner with a Confederate flag, so he put a watchdog on the island to keep trespassers at bay. One morning he awoke to see the Confederate flag flying from the mast. He rowed to the island, where

he found his watchdog dead. Weber cut down the Rebel flag, took it back to his cannon, loaded the gun with the flag and a substantial amount of powder, and blew it to pieces. Once again he raised the Stars and Stripes, and, lest the act go unnoticed, fired a 13-gun salute that was heard for miles around.

During the Civil War Stockton became the headquarters for the Third Regiment, California Volunteers of the United States of America, which established a camp in south Stockton at the site of the present McKinley Park. Captain Thomas E. Ketcham, Cheatham's old partner, was elected commanding officer of Company A.

By November of 1861 Camp McDoughal had become a quagmire because of rain on the adobe soil. The troops were moved to Benicia for the winter and returned the following spring in May of 1862. (They had been ordered back to Stockton to prepare for duty on the overland mail route across the northern plains and deserts.) The riverboat *Helen Hensley*, which carried the troops back to town, was greeted with a salute fired from Weber's cannon. The whole population of Stockton turned out to greet the boys. This time the regiment was established at Camp Halleck at the north end of the present San Joaquin County fairgrounds. The troops were made ready and the main body was moved out to Salt Lake City, leaving Companies A, B, and D behind. Company A, led by Ketcham, had just returned in triumph from the Indian war in Humboldt County and the men were the heroes of the day.

Company A was ordered to Fort Churchill in Nevada and Companies B and D to southern California. Stockton was left under the protection of the volunteer guards. Many of those who had taken up the Southern cause early in the Civil War now were gone. David S. Terry, Frank Cheatham, and others were no longer disrupting factors in the community. Many local Democrats remained loyal to the Union throughout the Civil War years, and thus the city emerged from the war on the winning side. It had survived the national conflict, maturing in the process. It was time for Stockton to move on to the business of doing business with the region's burgeoning new enterprise—agriculture.

IV.

THE CITY MATURES

By the latter half of the 19th century agriculture had become the primary economic force in the Great Valley. As more and more families settled on the rich farmland surrounding Stockton, the business of farming became the focus of the community's economic life. The manufacturing of farm machinery would soon become Stockton's number one industry. As early as 1851 a Stockton newspaper editor wrote of the necessity for inventiveness by farmers who would be successful in the Great Valley of California. He predicted failure for those who followed the old farming methods practiced in different terrains and climates—and success for the "men of larger intelligence" who would improve upon established practices.

One of the most significant innovations in California farming occurred in 1854 in the little-known blacksmith shop run by Perry Yaple and Wells Beardsley. They produced the first "improved gang of plows" in California. Yaple was serving his apprenticeship in Ithaca, New York in 1844 when the first patent for a gang plow was issued to T. Wiard in nearby East Avon. When Yaple completed his training he ran a blacksmith shop of his own until 1852 when he migrated to California. Yaple worked for the local stage company in Stockton for a year before opening his own shop with his friend, Beardsley, a wagonmaker who had traveled to California with him.

Years later Yaple would tell how he and Beardsley constructed the first three-bottom plows, with the three plow shares placed on a beam in tandem, offset from each other just enough to plow three rows at a time. With three horses hitched to one of these implements a man could plow a field in one third the time it took to complete the job with a single plow. These first plows received little public notice and their significance has been obscured in Stockton history. In 1858 Don Carlos Matteson, blacksmith, inventor, and manufacturer, developed and patented another improved plow of three shares, with wheels attached to support the weight of the implement. He renewed this same patent in 1868 when the plows had been developed even further. But Robert Baxter, a French Camp farmer who turned to manufacturing farm implements, must have been a better promoter, for he gained the attention of a Stockton *Daily Independent* reporter who wrote in June 1868:

There seems to be something in the atmosphere of San Joaquin County which excites the inventive talents and develops the latent genius of our citizens. The Matteson & Williamson and the Baxter gang plows have wrought a complete revolution in the mode of preparing the soil for cereals.

George H. Dahl of Stockton patented his "Samson" plow in 1868, claiming it was the strongest of all plows made and could hold as many shares as desired, depending on the type of soil being turned. In 1872 Samuel B. Bowen and Americus M. Abbott, both Stockton farm machinery manufacturers, secured a patent for a two-bottom plow constructed like a cart, complete with a seat which the plowman could ride upon behind the horses. Baxter sold first his plows and then his patent to the Webster

Washington School, Stockton's first high school, began in 1870 with A.H. Randall as the principal. The school was located at San Joaquin and Lindsey streets, serving for more than 30 years as the only public high school until Stockton High was built in 1940. The class of 1890 poses here on the front steps for their graduation picture. Courtesy, Pacific Center for Western Historical Studies, University of the Pacific

Employees of the Houser, Haines, and Knight Company gathered for a picture at the company's Aurora Street plant. The plant was destroyed by fire in 1888. Other farm manufacturing plants in the same vicinity were the Matteson & Williamson, Centennial Harvester Works, Shippee Harvest & Agricultural Works, and Holt Manufacturing. Courtesy, Pacific Center for Western Historical Studies, University of the Pacific

brothers' equipment supply store in Stockton. In 1872 Henry C. Shaw, a salesman for the store, purchased the company. He improved the Baxter plow and began the production of the Stockton Gang Plow, which would become famous around the world. The final improvement came when Matteson invented the first replaceable plow-share. The world of farming owed a great deal to these inventive men.

It is little wonder that the gang plow took on such importance in Stockton. By the mid-1870s most of the town's money came from the miles of golden grain fields that surrounded it. In 1873, 100,000 acres of wheat, 33,000 acres of barley, and 1,040 acres of oats were sown in the county alone. From 1854 to 1900 agriculture in the Great Valley was completely transformed. Where one man had plodded behind a single plow and a single horse to till a few acres, teams of horses pulling gang plows now worked hundreds of acres. The placing of multiple plows on one implement had opened the door to mechanized farming and Stockton businessmen soon were playing an important role in the development of the new industry. The city grew to include whole blocks of machine shops.

The invention of the gang plow initiated the demand for other farm equipment. Don Carlos Matteson and Thurman P. Williamson received patents for improvements on the Marvin Combined Harvester. They developed and perfected the Harvest Queen and Harvest King. Lodowich U. Shippee, farmer, merchant, and banker, put together the

The harvester-combine emancipated the large number of horses needed to draw the harvester. Often the 100-degree and higher temperatures in the San Joaquin Valley took the heaviest toll on the horses. By the 1880s the Stockton Wheel Company's combines made harvesting more efficient on the valley floor. Courtesy, Pacific Center for Western Historical Studies, University of the Pacific

Stockton Combined Harvest Agriculture Works, which built a successful combined harvester. The harvester was sold to Holt Bros. Manufacturing, who marketed it as the Holt Harvester. In 1893 five manufacturers in Stockton produced 450 various types of combined harvesters.

During the 1870s and 1880s wagon trains raised clouds of dust in the Great Valley as they hauled the grain into Stockton. Riverboats and barges transported commodities to San Francisco to be loaded on ships bound for Liverpool and other parts of the world. Within a very short time the Great Valley had become the breadbasket of the world.

The farmers soon found themselves confronted with monopolies in warehousing and shipping. They organized the Farmers' Cooperative Union in Stockton in 1873. The group put up $1,300 as starting capital, rented the Eureka Warehouses, and established an office. The cooperative proved to be an overwhelming success, netting over $600,000 worth of business in its first year of operation. The cooperative soon controlled the storage on the waterfront and became a strong influence in the city. In 1892 it also forced the lowering of shipping rates by supporting the Union Line, a competitive steamship company to the California Navigation and Improvement Company, which had monopolized the river traffic for several years.

The merchants of the city and the farmers of the county had long hoped that the construction of a railroad would help lower the cost of freighting, a vital factor in their economic survival. Dr. Erastus S. Holden, Stockton druggist and mayor of the city from 1859 to 1862, was a firm believer in the benefits of a railroad to the city, and was involved in organizational efforts to launch such a road.

The Railroad Convention held in San Francisco in 1859 had established San Francisco as the western terminus of the transcontinental railroad, but it was also agreed that the first section of the road would extend to Stockton through San Jose. The state legislature was to determine the route east from Stockton. Some planned to extend the road due east from Stockton over the Sierra, thus avoiding Sacramento. But Sacramento businessmen had other plans, and a classic power struggle began.

Perhaps Holden had the eastern route in mind when he organized the Stockton Copperopolis

Railroad. In the spring of 1863 a county-wide election failed to pass a bond issue to construct this road.

In the same election the voters did approve $250,000 in bonds for the Western Pacific Railroad (not the present company by that name) to build from San Francisco to Stockton and on to Sacramento. Although the railroad received $28,780 worth of the local bond money, not a cent was spent in the county. The company eventually went bankrupt and turned its assets over to the contractor, who sold it to the Central Pacific Railroad. The Central Pacific was under the control of the Sacramento businessmen known as the Big Four—Leland Stanford, Charles Crocker, Mark Hopkins, and Collis Huntington—who had no intentions of giving Stockton any of the business they intended for their own city.

After a vain attempt to establish a waterfront connection the railroad was finally constructed on Weber's county property just east of the city limits where the tracks run today, between Aurora and Union streets. On August 11, 1869 the first Western Pacific train arrived in Stockton—an excursion train

Above: The Holt Brothers began the Stockton Wheel Company in 1883 to capitalize on the five assets of the Stockton area—transportation, commerce, agricultural and industrial potential, and climate. The company's employees are seen at the factory on Aurora and Church streets. Ben Holt is at the extreme left in the first row. In 1892 the company was incorporated and renamed the Holt Manufacturing Company. Courtesy, Pacific Center for Western Historical Studies, University of the Pacific

Facing page, top: This view of the intersection of El Dorado and Main streets features the IXL general store on the left and the Holden Drug Store on the right. The electric street car, carbon-arc electric street lamps, and cobblestone road are evidence of the times and the changes to come in downtown Stockton. Courtesy, Stockton Public Library

Facing page, bottom: James E. Kidd opened his shop specializing in house, sign, and ornamental painting in the early 1870s at 228 N. El Dorado Street, and moved shortly thereafter to Main Street. The business remained in James Kidd's hands until 1924 when Joseph Kidd assumed the reins. Courtesy, Pacific Center for Western Historical Studies, University of the Pacific

of 42 cars loaded with visitors from Sacramento. The steam whistle shrilled as cheering men and women waved hats and handkerchiefs and church bells rang in celebration of the occasion. A parade proceeded down Weber Avenue before the Sacramento visitors scattered to prearranged gatherings.

In December 1870 the Stockton Copperopolis Railroad secured a right of way from the Stockton waterfront down Weber Avenue. The tracks were laid to Union Street and were connected to the Central Pacific tracks. By the end of the year the Central Pacific Railroad took over the Stockton Copperopolis Railroad, thus acquiring the waterfront connection it had hoped for. The company also tried to control river traffic but did not succeed.

Stockton businessmen began to realize that their city had become the supply base for all the San Joaquin Valley that lay to the south, and they took considerable interest in the formation of a railroad to serve these customers. There were two movements to establish such a railroad, one by the San Joaquin Valley Railroad, which was controlled by the backers of the Central Pacific, and the other by the Stockton Visalia Railroad, which was supported by the Stockton city council. The Stockton Visalia Railroad had been organized in part to counter the Central Pacific, which was becoming a monstrous monopoly.

The backers of both railroads asked the Stockton City Council to raise money for their projects. When Leland Stanford was questioned about the route of the San Joaquin Valley road and its connection to the Central Pacific-owned Western Pacific, he replied that the road might connect with the tracks leading to the Bay Area south of Stockton. A Stockton committee met with the company to look over the route of the road; Stanford's route was apparently not acceptable, for the city called for a bond issue of $300,000 to support the competitive Stockton Visalia Railroad. This time the bond issue passed and the new railroad was given a right of way down Hazelton Avenue. But the legality of the bond issue was questioned by opponents, perhaps backed by the Stanford group, and there were serious questions as to who paid the lawyers in the case. The court action delayed the project, eventually halting it. The road

was only constructed from the Copperopolis to Oakdale in Stanislaus County and was soon absorbed by the Southern Pacific, another Stanford controlled road.

Nonetheless the struggles between the "Big Four" monopoly (the Central Pacific, Western Pacific, Copperopolis, and Southern Pacific) and the city council continued. Stanford took revenge by building the Western Pacific Depot at Lathrop south of Stockton. Only tickets to San Francisco or Sacramento could be purchased locally; Stockton residents had to travel to San Francisco in order to get Pullman berth tickets for the East Coast even though every transcontinental train passed through town on the Western Pacific tracks. All westbound freight went to San Francisco first and then had to be shipped back to Stockton at additional costs.

This standoff between Stockton and the monopoly continued until 1898 when the Atchison, Topeka and Santa Fe Railroad finally brought the city what it needed most, a depot with a direct connection to the East Coast. The city also offered a grand welcome to the new Western Pacific when it arrived in 1910. Stockton thus became the only city in California to have three transcontinental railroad connections— the Southern Pacific, backed by the "Big Four," the Atchison, Topeka and Santa Fe, and the Western Pacific. Ironically, Stockton was the only city in the San Joaquin Valley that was not established by or at some time controlled by the railroads, in spite of Leland Stanford's efforts.

Although thousands of Chinese were recruited to work on the railroads, they had already been a part of Stockton community life for many years; their customs and language, however, often isolated them from the general population. The Stockton Chinese population was predominantly male, and a number of Chinese established businesses to cater to the bachelors' recreational appetites. Gambling houses, opium dens, and houses of prostitution were established, along with stores dealing in special foods and a Joss House, or shrine, all located in the original Chinatown in the area bounded by El Dorado, Channel, and Hunter streets, and Bridge Place.

Along with prostitutes, gamblers, and opium

dealers, the 1860 census lists the more numerous cooks, laundrymen, merchants, woodcutters, and laborers among the Chinese populace. By now a new Chinatown was emerging on El Dorado Street south of Market Street. In 1862 the old Chinatown burned to the ground. (The fire was not deliberately set, but the town's firemen were noticeably slow in responding to the fire call.) Before long most of the Chinese community moved to the area bounded by El Dorado, Market, Hunter, and Washington streets.

After the wave of Chinese who immigrated to build the railroads had completed the job, they looked for other means of earning a living. The census of 1880 showed that farm laborers outnumbered all other occupations in the Chinese population. Others who worked in town included woolen and paper mill workers, as well as domestic help. The Chinese were willing workers and hired out for less than Europeans and Americans. But in the

A typical wine and spirit shop on Main Street is depicted in the late 19th century. In addition to the sale of liquor, the shop also offered barrels of wine from local vintners. The wine was transferred into smaller kegs for customer convenience. Through the years many of the farms surrounding Stockton converted into vineyards, and a proliferation of vintners in the smaller towns added to Stockton's growth as the area's metropolis. Courtesy, M.A. Lawrence Collection

late 1800s a movement developed in the West to expel the Chinese from the United States. In 1882 David S. Terry, who had returned to Stockton after the Civil War, urged the U.S. Congress to stop Chinese immigration. The movement spread to Stockton, where eventually a petition was circulated to stop all immigration of the Chinese. The community's sentiments were mixed, for a Stockton newspaper printed a very favorable story about the consecration of a new Joss House, the Heungshen Temple, and the industrious character of the Chinese.

It was not long, however, before the politicians needing strong platforms took up the cry against the Chinese, and the press soon followed. The Federated Machinists and the Laborers' Union boycotted against businesses who hired Chinese. By March of 1886 the *Stockton Independent* became disenchanted with the movement when the Laborers' Union leader called for a boycott of the newspaper because of its lack of endorsement of all the union's activities.

It was, however, the farmers who came to the rescue of the Chinese. The Stockton Grange No. 7, Patrons of Husbandry denounced the boycotts as "un-American, unjust, tyrannical and opposed to our laws of free institution." The group also condemned the California press for "encouraging the evil passion of the worst elements of Society." Since most of the valley's Chinese were working on farms, it is apparent that the agricultural community did not want to be boycotted for hiring them.

Sylvia Sun Minnick, in her 1983 thesis on the San Joaquin County Chinese, summed up the conditions in the Stockton Chinese community during this trying period:

It is without doubt the 1885-86 anti-Chinese campaign was the major reason that the Chinese laundry business as well as the other Chinese occupations declined in Stockton and within the county. The campaign itself was not a total success; but the fact that Stockton did not experience any major violent incident is a credit to her community leaders. Foremost in the minds of all those who worked against the Chinese was that any action taken had to be within the legal system; that philosophy, in spite of racist feelings, demonstrates the people's respect for the law.

Ironically, respect for the law sometimes eluded the town's first citizens. In his later years Charles M. Weber, the city's benefactor, experienced frustrations that sometimes led to irrational actions on his part. He had worked continually to protect not only his land but the whole city from floods. He constructed canals along both East and North streets to divert

Facing page, top: Work began for the spectacular wood and glass Agricultural Pavilion in 1887 and was completed the following year at a cost of $50,000. The building occupied one square block bounded by Washington, Lafayette, Hunter, and San Joaquin streets, otherwise known as Washington Square. Courtesy, Mel Bennett

Facing page, bottom: In the early morning light of September 29, 1902, Stock-tonians saw only rubble and twisted metal on Washington Square, the result of a devastating fire which destroyed the beautiful 39,000-square-foot Agri-cultural Pavilion, and took the life of fireman Tom Walsh. Courtesy, Pacific Center for Western Historical Studies, University of the Pacific

floodwaters. He raised the levees along both Stockton and Mormon sloughs and built a bulkhead on the latter at Stanislaus Street. Yet he did not succeed in convincing the city leaders to complete the project. This frustration, along with the constant harrassment he endured from people who tore down the fences around his property in order to let their livestock graze on his land, led him to take potshots at tres-passers, including mischievous boys. On one such occasion a youngster broke an arm in his efforts to escape. This led the *Stockton Independent* to editorialize about Weber in April of 1877:

Captain C.M. Weber, the pioneer founder of our city, is a man of ungovernable temper and of so many peculiar and eccentric freaks of character that his best friends are at all times at a loss to know in what new form his eccentricities will manifest themselves. While he is one of the most generous men in the world, he is peculiarly sensitive about being imposed upon and a trespassing cow on his property will put him in more of a rage than would a more serious matter.

Weber invited the editor to meet with him and told him of his frustrations in getting the city to act. He had done more than his part, he believed, and he expected the city government to do its share in protecting the downtown. The editor printed Weber's comments and agreed that anyone might be as frustrated under similar circumstances, but did not

Left: Although floods occurred frequently in Stockton, snowfall was a rarity. This picturesque scene of the first courthouse taken after the January 28, 1880, snowstorm serves as a reminder of this phenomenal event of the past that few can recall and documents seldom record. Courtesy, Pacific Center for Western Historical Studies, University of the Pacific

Above: The second San Joaquin County Court House, constructed of brick and faced with marble, was completed in 1891 at a total cost of $278,850. The contractor received additional money for the project by erecting a high fence around the entire lot, charging 10 cents to every sidewalk superintendent who wanted to watch the construction. Courtesy, San Joaquin County Historical Museum

retract his remarks about Weber's temperament. It was true that Weber no longer socialized and led a reclusive life during his later years. His one pleasure seemed to be gardening. His health deteriorated and although he was in great pain during his last few months he refused to take morphine. He died of pneumonia on May 3, 1881, and was buried on the following Saturday.

The Stockton City Council adopted a resolution suspending all business in the city at one o'clock on the day of the funeral. St. Mary's Church was overflowing for the funeral Mass. The procession—led by over 500 men representing the fire department, various societies, and military groups—marched from the church. The horse-drawn hearse was followed by over 100 carriages. Everyone in Stockton was represented; the last four carriages were filled with Weber's friends from Chinatown. Weber himself might have been surprised at the size of the crowd that came to pay tribute. The populace finally gave him the recognition he must have believed he deserved.

By the mid-1880s the town was growing up, and its institutions, as well as its citizenry, matured. The older men in the volunteer fire companies—which had traditionally been social and political organizations—spoke of the need for a paid fire department. The younger men joining the fire companies volunteered as much for fun as for firefighting. With more incendiary fires occurring, the need for a dependable team increased. According to one local historian, it was the firemen themselves who set many of these fires, presumably to beat competitive companies to the scene. "At some of these fires liquor was freely passed around and some of the firemen became staggering drunk." In 1887 the volunteer companies joined in requesting that the city council establish a paid fire department, which they finally did in August 1888.

Stockton took on a new look during the summer of 1888 when the block-long Agricultural Pavilion was constructed on Washington Square. It was the largest building in town, and certainly one of the most beautiful, and was used for many community activities. At night the lights in its dome could be

Built in 1893, the San Joaquin County Jail on San Joaquin and Channel streets was dubbed "Cunningham's Castle" in honor of Thomas Cunningham, who served as sheriff for almost 30 years. Because the jail was originally constructed to house only 75 prisoners, overcrowding and lack of sanitation facilities forced its closure by 1959 and new facilities were built in French Camp. Courtesy, San Joaquin County Historical Museum

seen for miles. The handsome building stood for 14 years until it burned in a raging fire that consumed the structure within an hour.

For some time city leaders had discussed the need for a new courthouse, but in 1885 the question of title to the land arose once again. The city lacked funds to spend on such an ambitious project, so the county filed an action to obtain a clear title. The court ruled that the land remained the property of the Weber heirs but that the public held the easement as long as the property was used for public purposes.

The ruling declared that the city still held a half-interest in improvements on the property, so a compromise was worked out in which the city turned over its share of the interest to the county in

exchange for 15 years' rent in designated rooms of the new building. Thus the second courthouse, the grandest in California, constructed of brick and faced with California granite, was completed in December 1890 on Block 3, or Court House Square.

In 1893 a new jail was also constructed. The red brick structure, of an unusual medieval design, was known to four generations as Cunningham's Castle. Thomas Cunningham, who influenced the building's design, served as county sheriff for almost 30 years, from 1871 to 1899. He had been a Stockton city councilman and was highly respected both locally and in California law circles.

By the 1890s Stockton had become an industrial city. A California magazine article published in 1893 discussed local manufacturers and their workers:

They employ an army of 1,300 operatives to whom they pay $1,000,000 annually and a large proportion of the earnings are invested in home building. The result is that Stockton breadwinners are largely also homeowners, and the proportion of pretty cottages and even more pretentious residences owned by wage-workers in this city is hardly excelled in any city in the United States.

Above: The 1890 July Fourth parade makes its way westward along Weber Avenue. This picture was taken from the courthouse and shows a good view of the Capitol Hotel (the Mansion House), the Tretheway Building (the Argonaut Hotel), and the Hammond and Yardley Grocery Store. The Tin House and Weber Baths are to the extreme left, and behind them is the Masonic Temple with flags flying on the roof. Courtesy, Pacific Center for Western Historical Studies, University of the Pacific

Facing page, top: Franklin Grammar School was built in 1859 at Center and Washington streets and torn down 100 years later. Better known as Center Street School, it served as the educational institution for the town's ethnic minority communities. Chinese and Japanese children attended Franklin School exclusively during times of racial tension in the early decades of the 20th century. Courtesy, Pacific Center for Western Historical Studies, University of the Pacific

Facing page, bottom: The Fremont Grammar School at Aurora and Fremont streets held a Columbus Day celebration in 1892 for parents and local residents. The school opened in 1890 and was temporarily closed the following year because of a diphtheria scare. The belltower became the subject of much ridicule until it was removed in 1911. Courtesy, Pacific Center for Western Historical Studies, University of the Pacific

Many of the finer homes in Stockton were actually the second homes of farmers who did not want their families isolated on farms during the winter when the roads were too muddy to travel. Town homes also made it possible for farm children to attend the more convenient city schools.

Stockton's increasing maturity was reflected in the pressure that population growth caused in the city school system. In 1870 teacher Ambrose H. Randall saw the need for an extended educational system and started a high school in the front rooms of Stockton School District's Washington School. Classes were held there until 1904 when Stockton High School

This home belonged to the assistant physician of the State Insane Asylum and was located on the institution's grounds. A two-story brick structure, the house had many windows which provided ample ventilation to cool the residents during Stockton's heat waves. Courtesy, Stockton Development Center

was built at the corner of California and Vine streets. Among the high school's first graduates were Lottie and Ewald Carl Grunsky, the eldest children of early settler Charles Grunsky. The graduates were awarded teaching certificates with their diplomas. Lottie began teaching immediately and spent most of her life working in the Stockton school system. The Lottie Grunsky School, built in 1919 in east Stockton, was named for her. Young Carl taught locally for one year

and then went to Germany to complete his education. He received a degree in engineering and returned to California where he pursued a distinguished career in state, city, and federal water projects, including the Panama Canal and the Port of Stockton.

During the 1850s the few black children in town had been welcomed into the school system but by 1860 political pressure had forced these children into a private school. The "Colored School" was incorporated into the Stockton school district in 1863 but was still operated as a segregated facility. In 1876 a black student was refused entry into the high school and was sent to San Francisco to complete his studies. But within two years the first blacks were admitted into the high school and in 1879 the Stockton School

District "Colored School" was closed and all went to regular schools. The first Japanese student, George Katsumi Kusano, graduated from Stockton High School in 1895. It was not until 1899 that the first Chinese student, Guy Tye, was allowed into a class, but he was soon followed by other Chinese entering the Stockton school system. Unfortunately the Chinese students would not be the last to face prejudice in the schools; they were, however, apparently the last ones openly refused admittance. As intolerant as this seems, Stockton was more than 20 years ahead of San Francisco in allowing Chinese students into the public school system.

In the years preceding the turn of the century Stockton's boundaries grew to the south and east. Gaslights of an earlier era were replaced by electric lights. Horse-drawn streetcars were replaced by electric trolleys. Some city streets that had been paved with planks and gravel were now paved with basalt blocks and granite curbs. Others were graveled.

As the city moved into the 20th century, Stockton became known for its hospitals for the mentally ill. In addition to the State Insane Asylum, another institution, the Pacific Asylum, was established by Dr. Asa Clark, who eventually became superintendent of the state asylum. Clark was one of many early residents whose contributions helped shape the young city.

The story of one such resident, Charles Grunsky, typifies the stories of Stockton's pioneer settlers. Grunsky had been a participant in the city's growth almost from its beginnings. He had made a fortune while engaged in business with the miners, but returned to his home in Germany to claim a bride, then settled down to raise his family in Stockton. In 1856 he became the president and main moving force in the Turnverein, a German athletic and social group. His early fortune dwindled away, mostly because of an unfortunate selection of partners in a variety of businesses, including farming, of which he knew little. He had also been politically active and held numerous public offices. He was at one time or another harbor master, city auditor, and county recorder. Though he was a cut above the ordinary citizen, his problems were the same as those

During city celebrations in the 1900s the Main Street entrance and the dome of the courthouse were outlined by hundreds of individual incandescent electric lights that relayed a festive message to all the town's citizens. Stock- tonians referred to the spectacular illumination as a "blaze of light, turning night into day." Courtesy, Pacific Center for Western Historical Studies, University of the Pacific

experienced by many men of the times. He lost his first two wives to tuberculosis and two children died in infancy. His third wife had been widowed, and he helped raise her two children. He was a family man who taught his children self-respect and responsibility. In his later years he saw three of his sons marry, and lived to see five of his grandchildren born. Grunsky died in August of 1891, 52 years after arriving in Stockton.

By the time the 20th century approached, Stockton had changed. Besides founding fathers like Grunsky and Weber, settlers such as David S. Terry, Thomas Cunningham, and many of the other early pioneers were dead. The city entered a new era with new pioneers in charge.

V.

CHANGING TIMES

The city of Stockton was undergoing many changes at the beginning of the 20th century. Growth and changes in farming brought changes to the city as well, and the busy port that had served the mines now serviced the farms.

Local farming had begun with the production of grain and hay to feed livestock; later the grain was exported to cities around the world. Vegetables and fruit were grown locally to feed the local population, but, with the coming of the railroads, valley farmers found they could ship produce out to a greater area. Thus new types of farming developed. As emigrants came into the area, settling on small parcels of land, intensive farming became the valley's new direction. Orchards, vineyards, and truck gardens required various types of machinery, so the town's machine shops built new equipment for tilling, harvesting, and processing farm products. Canneries were established near the source of supply and provided employment for local women outside their homes.

Around 1900 a new influx of Italians came to Stockton—although there had always been Italians in the city, for some had emigrated during the Gold Rush. Gaetano Alegretti's grocery and saloon became a gathering place for the new emigrants. Alegretti, who had opened his Stockton store in 1869, was fluent in English, French, and Spanish, and was often asked to write letters home for those who could not write. He became the new arrivals' advisor and friend. He encouraged the Italian farmers to organize a "mutual benefit society," suggesting they restrict their membership to men who were both farmers and Italians. In 1902 he helped them set up the organization even though he was not eligible for membership under the rules. They named the group *Societa Italiana Dei Gardinieri,* (the Italian Gardeners' Society). They soon elected officers and the group began to grow, forming a strong organization that would one day be their salvation. The Italian Gardeners took up farming in several rural locations near Stockton, but those in closest proximity lived in the area between the north edge of Stockton and the Calaveras River.

As the small parcels of land were farmed north of Stockton, the delta west of the city was also developed. The delta soil is a light, fluffy peat of decomposed vegetation, so completely organic it will burn. This land required new machines and Stockton's inventors met the challenge. Robert Baxter had experimented and built a successful ditching plow for the light peat soil as early as 1860. The Samson Iron Works built marine and stationary engines to pump out the surplus water in the delta fields, and the Stockton Iron Works manufactured clamshell diggers to replace Chinese laborers in the construction of levees.

As the need for local river transportation increased, William Colberg established a fleet of small boats to service the isolated farms. He carried passengers and light freight for pay, but delivered the mail free for many years until the company received a government contract in 1928. Before 1900 he started a boat works to keep his fleet in shape and expanded it into an extensive shipbuilding operation, Colberg Boat Works, which became Colberg Inc. in 1960. The firm is still operating today.

A dramatic skyline view of Stockton in the 1930s shows the growing businesses in the downtown section. The court-house dome on the left towers over the magnificent Hotel Stockton at the head of the Stockton Channel. The body of water to the right is McLeod Lake. Courtesy, Pacific Center for Western Historical Studies, University of the Pacific

By the turn of the century steam tractors began to replace horses, but in order to keep the heavy machines from sinking into the light delta soil their wheels were made wider and wider. Benjamin Holt kept increasing the size of the wheels on his steam tractors until they were 16 feet wide. In 1904 Holt put his men to work re-designing track-laying wheels that would more evenly distribute the weight of the tractors. The first improved "tracks" were installed on a standard steam traction engine during the winter of 1905. Holt tested the model in the delta soil and several were sold commercially, having to prove themselves on the job. Because steam engines were so heavy Holt experimented with gasoline engines and in 1906 produced his first model, Number 1001. A Stockton photographer, Charles Clements, named the contraption when he remarked, "it crawls like a caterpillar." Holt liked the description and used the name. Thus the Caterpillar tractor, the machine that would help change the face of the world, was born in Stockton.

One of the most successful early delta farmers was a Japanese, George Shima, of Stockton. He was a shrewd but fair businessman and was highly respected in Stockton, despite ill feelings toward many of his countrymen due to a statewide anti-Japanese movement created by organized labor. In 1892 San Francisco labor leader Dennis Kearny had planted the seeds of opposition as he declared the Japanese would "demoralize and disorganize the labor market." A local newspaper claimed the Japanese attitude had become arrogant after Japan won the Russo-Japanese War in 1905. But the mistrust of the Japanese more often stemmed from the fact that they were, as a group, frugal and industrious, saving their money and venturing into farming for themselves. They recognized the value of the delta soil for farming, but they were also willing to live in the delta, which was isolated by the lack of roads. Many of their farms could be reached only by water. A pro-Japanese association was organized in Stockton in 1907 but that was soon countered by the formation, in 1908, of a local chapter of the statewide Exclusion League, organized to keep Japanese out of the country. The

Facing page: Unloading a barge of bricks is representative of waterfront activities, the Stockton Channel playing a key role in transportation and town development. Paying only 50 cents for a one-way fare, passengers waited at the waterfront to board steamers bound for San Francisco. A marvelous view of the Masonic Temple, which was built in 1883 and razed in 1931, is also featured in this photograph. Courtesy, Stockton Public Library

Above: Founded in 1902, the Italian Gardeners Society has been the leading organization to perpetuate Stockton's Italian culture. The group's popular annual picnic was held at Bide-A-Wee Park at Wilson Way and Main Street in 1911. Courtesy, Tillio Boggiano

Right: A river schooner, sometimes referred to as a mud scow, gracefully makes its way on the San Joaquin River in 1907. Also known as the workhorses of the river, the schooners were commonly used for hauling bricks, sand, wheat, and barley. Courtesy, Glenn A. Kennedy

state Alien Land Law of 1913, which excluded
ownership of land by those not eligible for
citizenship, was directly aimed at these farmers.
Additional restrictive laws were passed in 1920 and
1923, but many Japanese continued to lease land and
farm around Stockton or establish businesses in town
until World War II.

Many Stockton residents were startled awake early
on April 18, 1906 by the sound of chimney bricks
crashing down on their rooftops. But minor damage
in the city was soon forgotten as news of the
devastation in San Francisco spread throughout the
community. Citizens immediately mobilized to
provide help in the form of both money and supplies.
By the following day a steamer left Stockton with
1,500 blankets from the Stockton Woolen Mills,
600 sacks of potatoes, 2,000 loaves of bread, and
several hundred sacks of flour, as well as thousands of
gallons of milk for the homeless in San Francisco.
Each bakery in town baked 2,000 extra loaves of
bread; half was sent by rail to Oakland and San
Francisco and the remainder was used for refugees
who came pouring into Stockton. Schoolchildren
took food to the supply boat that left the docks for
San Francisco each afternoon. One man offered a cow
a day as long as needed, and the Aurora Flour Mill
donated 20 barrels of flour daily for the homeless in
San Francisco.

Eight thousand dollars was immediately raised for
relief and a number of local men went to the
devastated city to help out. Two companies of the
local National Guard were ordered to San Francisco.
Households in Stockton were urged to share extra
beds in their homes, and the Chamber of Commerce
office became a clearing house for refugees. Refugee
centers were established in the local halls, and church
groups served meals. Everyone helped where they
could, and Stockton once again became a magnet city,
drawing people from San Francisco just as it had
during the Gold Rush. City folks who had deridingly
called Stockton "Mudville" suddenly found it a
haven. A need had arisen and the people had
responded, welcoming the homeless and providing a
helping hand.

Stockton had escaped earthquake damage, but in

The Colberg fleet of small
boats tied up to the head of the
Stockton Channel serviced the
isolated delta farming
communities, carrying
passengers, light freight, and
mail. By 1928 Colberg
received a government contract
for delivering the mail,
although until that time he
had been providing the service
for free. The stern-wheeler tied
up alongside of the launches is
the J.P. Peters. Courtesy,
Stockton Chamber of
Commerce

March of 1907 disaster struck in the form of a
devastating flood. Most of the city went under water
deeper than ever before. Some areas were under three
feet of water as the Calaveras, Mormon Slough, and
even the Stockton Channel overflowed. The city had
been plagued with frequent flooding during the wet
years of the 1850s, and even greater destruction
occurred during the flood of 1862, which turned the
Great Valley into a lake. This flood had so
immobilized the city that no one could move about
except in boats. Men wading through the streets in
hip boots were apt to step into deep holes caused by
raging water currents that made channels of the
streets. After the water receded, the city lay covered
in two to three inches of silt. Weber's beautiful
garden on the Point was destroyed and never
completely recovered. In 1871-1872 and 1889-1890
major floods again created havoc. In 1903, 1904, and
1906 parts of the city were under water again.

The root of Stockton's flooding problems lay at the
juncture of the Calaveras River and Mormon Slough

Above: Relentlessly conscious of strikes and labor conflicts in the early years of the century, small Stockton businesses continued to give personal service. Here an employee of the American Fish and Oyster Company makes a home delivery to the Volpi house on Washington Street. Courtesy, M.A. Lawrence Collection

Right: Aside from the many people working on farms, in industrial plants, and local businesses, Stockton also had the independent tradesman. Here a Hunter Street vendor waits patiently at his wagon for customers needing their knives and tools sharpened. The building in the background is the Masonic Temple. Courtesy, Pacific Center for Western Historical Studies, University of the Pacific

in an area 16 miles northeast of the city at Bellota. Mormon Slough had at one time originated in the foothills three miles south of the Calaveras at Bellota. The Calaveras had created an alluvial fan that acted as a natural earth dam and diverted the stream in a sharp turn at that point. Only at very high flood stage did the water spill over this natural barrier and into a series of normally "dry washes" that eventually led into Mormon Slough.

What had taken nature years to build, man managed to destroy in a short time. A few farmers, through a series of manipulations, had inadvertently managed to divert the Calaveras River flow into Mormon Slough. The slough was not big enough to carry the water so it overflowed its banks. As time

went on, silt began to block the slough's entrance into Stockton Channel and made the situation in Stockton worse. As early as 1902 a state senate committee recommended the construction of a diverting canal east of Stockton to take the water out of Mormon Slough and put it back into the Calaveras, but the federal government controlled the waterways and bureaucratic action was slow.

The massive destruction of the 1907 flood served to counteract the inertia of the bureaucrats, and by November of that year it was announced the right-of-way was finally secured for the planned Diverting

Canal. Work started at Bellota but in January of 1909 the city was again flooded while workers toiled on the Mormon Slough levees east of town. Rumors spread that men from the north side of the slough in Stockton planned to cut the south levee to protect themselves. The south-siders patrolled their levee with shovels and guns to prevent this dastardly deed from occurring, and the city split into factions. Whether the rumor was true or not, an unhealthy climate of distrust pervaded the city. Nonetheless, the Diverting Canal was completed in 1911.

In the early years of this century, the labor movement made strides in organizing the workers of the Stockton manufacturing center. There were strikes against Holt Manufacturing, Stockton Iron Works, and the Globe Foundry during 1903 and 1904. The M.M. & E. (Merchants, Manufacturers and Employees Association), the Millers and Warehousemen's Association, and Sperry Mills supported the management position. The Feed and Flour Packers joined the strikers. By the time the workers in the city finally went back to work there

Floods continued to plague Stockton well into the 20th century. This view of San Joaquin Street looking northward provides a good picture of the front and upstairs porch of the Columbia House at the northwest corner of the inter- *section. Also visible are wooden sidewalks, a flooded pedestrian footbridge, and citizens checking the depth of the water. Courtesy, Pacific Center for Western Historical Studies, University of the Pacific*

had been considerable damage done to labor-management relations in the community.

From 1905 to 1914 labor conflicts were marked by violence. Most labor stoppages had been initiated by the labor movement, but on July 8, 1914 blaring headlines greeted Stocktonians: "Merchants, Manufacturers and Employers Association declares for open shop in Stockton. Stockton Millmen told to go to work under open shop or get their pay." Non-union men were brought from San Francisco to replace the fired workers. Private guards escorted the men aboard the steamer into Stockton.

Before long the city was paralyzed as every union in

Top: Built in 1916 at Harding Way and Pacific Avenue, El Dorado School continues to stand as an example of Elizabethan Tudor architecture. Although this picture was taken during Girls' Play Day, the boys watching out the second floor windows show that everyone could enjoy the activities. Courtesy, Stockton Chamber of Commerce

Above: Although the San Joaquin County Hospital and Almshouse entrance may look rather bleak, the hospital itself is rich in history. The establishment began at the East Street (Wilson Way) complex in 1856, and in 1892 all the buildings burned to the ground, luckily without the loss of a single life. The hospital moved to the 400-acre parcel in French Camp just south of Stockton in 1895, where the hospital remains today. Courtesy, Glenn A. Kennedy

town got involved when they refused to cross picket lines and boycotted M.M. & E. Association members. Irving Martin of the *Stockton Record* editorialized, discussing the starvation and devastation being wrought by the war in Europe. He continued, "here in Stockton under smiling skies surrounded by bountiful crops with plenty to spare for every man— here we are destroying every relation that makes individual happiness and community prosperity possible." He pleaded for arbitration to settle the city's problems, caused by 900 workers who refused to work in open shops or who were locked out of their jobs for refusing to cross picket lines. Martin later gave testimony at a hearing before a Federal Committee of Industrial Relations in San Francisco, and, when asked his opinion of what was happening in Stockton, gave this assessment:

This situation in Stockton in my judgment is not only union and non-union. It is far deeper and broader than that. It is absolutely a class situation. It is absolutely the employers and financiers on one side and those who work on the other. The class lines are just as absolutely drawn as anything can be. This is a fight of class against class.

It was Christmas of 1914 before the strike was settled, with both sides agreeing to go to a committee for arbitration in the future. This did not end the labor disputes, but they were never quite as serious or violent again.

Despite Stockton's labor problems the city continued to grow at a rapid pace. If a person had taken a riverboat out of Stockton in 1900 and not returned for 30 years, he would have had difficulty in recognizing the city, for the skyline had completely changed—dramatic evidence of a dynamic era.

In 1902 the Stockton Savings and Loan Society (now Bank of Stockton) started a new trend when it announced plans for Stockton's first skyscraper. The building was completed in 1906 and still stands on the northeast corner of San Joaquin and Main streets. The following year city boosters thrilled to the announcement of a new elegant tourist hotel of "Spanish Renaissance" style, to be constructed on Weber's Hole, a former channel lot at the head of Stockton Slough between El Dorado and Hunter streets. The construction contract for the new Hotel Stockton was signed in 1908, and the project, largely funded by local investors, was completed and dedicated in 1910. The new hotel dominated the head of the channel, permanently changing the Stockton skyline. In 1910 the Hotel Stockton became the showplace of the valley, with a roof garden that gave a dramatic view of Mount Diablo, especially on warm summer evenings when the sun set as a fiery red ball. The city council, which had finally used up its free rent in the county courthouse, moved into the hotel's second floor annex. Ironically, the councilmen ended up as tenants in a building on the site Weber had offered them years before.

Five high-rise buildings were constructed in downtown Stockton between 1910 and 1917. The most prolific designer of commercial buildings in Stockton was the architectural firm of Glenn Allen and Charles H. Young. Either individually or collectively Allen and Young were responsible for the Clark, the Wolf, and three other hotels; major apartment projects; eight commercial structures; seven warehouses and garages; three lodge buildings; two grammar schools, including the Lottie Grunsky School, and the Municipal Baths and Civic Memorial Auditorium.

Above: New subdivisions developed within the city limits, and many of the homes were single-family dwellings. Here a family at one such dwelling is seen enjoying a respite in the late afternoon. Courtesy, M.A. Lawrence Collection

Facing page, top: As more county roads and city streets were paved, the automobile became Stockton's primary mode of transportation. A wealthy Chinese cannery owner even purchased a fleet of Model "T" trucks to transport both cannery workers and produce at the Althouse-Eagal Fordson Company on El Dorado

Street. Courtesy, Pacific Center for Western Historical Studies, University of the Pacific

Facing page, bottom: The Number 12 car ran on Main and El Dorado streets. By 1892 the Stockton Street Railroad Company switched from horse-drawn cars to 10-horsepower electric cars. These electric cars built in local industrial plants were fairly small in size and held a total of 28 passengers per car. Courtesy, San Joaquin County Historical Museum

Residential development was just as active as commercial development during this progressive period of Stockton's history. Subdivisions cropped up in every direction. The real estate firm of Otto Grunsky and F.J. "Joe" Dietrich sold property aggressively, advertising in a wide variety of publications as diverse as the U.S. Navy magazine and

Italian newspapers. The firm sold property for as little as 1/48th down payment, "three dollars down and three dollars a month," according to one young realtor. The company developed several housing tracts including the Oaks, Brookside, Bours Park, Mossdale, Northcrest, Burkett Acres, and North, all in the immediate vicinity of Stockton. Before 1914 five more subdivisions were developed by others. In 1914 the city annexed North, Fair Oaks, and the Homestead area south of the city. The city was in the midst of a remarkable building boom that year and a Stockton reporter waxed with enthusiasm:

Think of it! Stockton ranked ahead of New York, San Francisco and all the other metropolitan centers of the United States, ahead of every city in the nation in building permits.

Transportation was a key to the changes wrought in the city of Stockton. By 1900 there were four electric streetcar lines that covered the city from north to south and east to west. By 1906 the system had doubled in size. In 1910 the streetcar lines were purchased by the Central California Traction Company, which ran 48 interurban trips a day in Stockton and north of the city to Sacramento. The Stockton Terminal and Eastern Railroad also offered service to the area northeast of the city to the farming community of Linden.

Public transportation encountered new competition, however, as improved city streets and county roads made automobiles more desirable. The city police department purchased a motorized ambulance and the fire department its first trucks in 1912. The police added a motorcycle in 1914, and the following year there were 1,152 automobiles in Stockton alone—not surprising, perhaps, in a city that had always been a transportation hub.

There was a great deal of entertainment available for the city during this time. There were traveling shows including Wild West shows and circuses, as well as local celebrations. There were stock company performances and Grand Opera. Appearances by as wide a variety of celebrities as prizefighters Jim Jefferies and John Sullivan, theatrical stars Ethel

The Hammond and Yardley Grocery Store, shown here in the 1910s, was one of the places patrons congregated in to exchange daily news. It was an ideal location, situated at 300 E. Weber Avenue, opposite the courthouse. Courtesy, Dohrman King

Barrymore, Al Jolson, Sarah Bernhardt, Marie Dressler, and Will Rogers were enjoyed by Stocktonians. In 1919 the County Fair was revived at Oak Park and was soon moved to the fairgrounds on Charter Way where a building was constructed in 1921. Horse races, automobile races, and demonstrations of that thrilling new invention, the aeroplane, took place on the fairgrounds.

Local movie fans flocked to the movie theater to see *The Whistle,* a William S. Hart film made in Stockton. In 1921 Stockton Radio pioneered as the Portable Wireless Telegraph Company (KWG Radio), which inaugurated a cooperative news service with the *Stockton Record.* Today KWG is the second oldest commercial station in California.

Stockton has always been a sports town with plenty of local participation. Baseball has always been popular. Babe Ruth played an exhibition game at Oak Park on October 23, 1924. Basketball was popular at the YMCA's new gymnasium. There was boxing, until the Women's Christian Temperance Union and churches got the city council to force boxing out of the city limits and into the county. Boys had always found places to swim in the sloughs and river but Yosemite Lake became the favorite spot in 1916. It was not only the place to swim but also the place to be seen. The Mineral Baths, which were eventually purchased by the city and became a public spa,

offered a full day of relaxation for the city's workers. Skating rinks had long been popular in town, and there were always dances, church socials, and school picnics to attend.

Saloons and houses of prostitution remained a part of the city, as they had been since Gold Rush days. Perhaps the most famous house was the "Bull Pen," constructed in Chinatown in 1905. It was located in the heart of the block; the actual spot can be seen today as the promenade called Chang Wah Lane located between Hunter and El Dorado streets. There was sporadic discussion of the vice in the local newspapers, but little was done until the state passed the Red Light Law in 1913. This provided a legal means for closing the Bull Pen and other such houses, but many prostitutes moved into at least one downtown hotel and the surrounding residential districts.

Liquor had become the target of a major anti-vice campaign at the turn of the century so prostitution continued under less scrutiny. Temperance leader Carry Nation and her vigorous campaign had not gone unnoticed, for children were being taught about the evils of "demon rum" in Stockton's schools and churches. The populace voted for Sunday closings of saloons but a second vote soon reopened them. When

The Anteros Club, a young bachelor club, performed many amateur plays between 1902 and the 1920s. Many important local names have been members and performers, such as Asa Clark, Dave Mathews, Henry Yost, Joe Gail, Warren Atherton, and Otto Sandman. Here the club members are enjoying a hayride on Sutter Street in 1905. Courtesy, Pacific Center for Western Historical Studies, University of the Pacific

California became the 29th state to ratify the 18th amendment speakeasies became as common in Stockton as in other parts of the country. There were reported to be as many as 23 illegal establishments in Stockton in an equal number of days after Prohibition went into effect. Home brew recipes were a dime a dozen and hundreds of homes became do-it-yourself breweries. G-men caught Stockton's share of moonshiners. As the city cracked down on illegal operations regular jitney services took patrons to the roadhouses out of town. Though Prohibition was a joke to some it was serious business to many who tried to enforce the law. Bad liquor had made some ill and killed others in town. Prohibition was no different in Stockton than in other places. Probably the greatest harm it did was give the average citizen a reason to break the law.

The community had been reminded about the war

Top: Two young men are depicted in this 1910 photo relaxing in the park in suits and derbies. The dress code was far more formal compared with today's standards. Courtesy, M.A. Lawrence Collection

Above: The Mineral Baths on South San Joaquin Street, first named Jackson Natural Gas Well Baths, were later named the McKinley Park and Pool. In the hot summers people flocked to the baths for a swim, a picnic under the trees, for band concerts, or to ride the scenic railway, making it the most popular place in the 1920s and 1930s. Courtesy, Pacific Center for Western Historical Studies, University of the Pacific

Above right: A local Stockton beauty, clad in her black silk dress and light color parasol, poses before the camera in 1905. Courtesy, M.A. Lawrence Collection

Facing page: Young boys dreaded church because they had to don their Sunday best. Here Roy A. Kennedy manages a half-hearted smile in spite of his clothes. Courtesy, Glenn A. Kennedy

in Europe during the labor strike in 1914 but that war was far away to most Stocktonians. The conflict in Mexico had much more impact, especially when the men of the Stockton Unit of the National Guard were the first troops sent to Nogales after Pancho Villa's raid. But the European conflict was more important to Stockton than most local people realized, as the Holt Brothers' Caterpillar attracted the attention of the military. The U.S. Army tested one of the machines by pulling an artillery piece through the mud; it proved equal to the job but unfortunately the army had no money to buy the equipment. Finally a British Army officer developed an idea for an armored vehicle, an idea he borrowed from a friend who had observed a Caterpillar at work. Benjamin Holt was contacted and agreed to send specifications for the under-carriage and to manufacture his engines for a new machine. Great security was placed around the assembly plant. The public was told the new machines would be used to transport water to the army in Egypt. Reservoirs soon became "tanks" in the vernacular of the workmen.

Next a rumor spread that the machines were snowplows to be used in Russia. This was squelched when an eight-inch Howitzer was added and the crawlers moved into battle. The British Armored Motorcars were the turning point in World War I. High ranked British officers credited Benjamin Holt with winning the war. The *Stockton Independent* covered the story.

Now comes word that these armoured motorcars are nothing more or less than the Holt Caterpillar, the product of a Stockton man's dream; little did he think when he produced his track laying tractor a few years ago to make possible the cultivation of lands too soft to be profitable when tilled by horses that his invention would be one of the world's greatest military assets.

On March 6, 1917 the country officially went to war against Germany. The announcement was followed, in Stockton, by an immediate effort to raise money with a Liberty Loan bond drive. With 2,400 workers at the Holt Manufacturing plant drawing an

annual payroll of two and a half million dollars, there was little difficulty raising money for the war effort. Every bond drive exceeded expectations.

Selective service registration was instituted with 365 men designated as Stockton's quota. Before the local recruits left town a parade was held in their honor. Stockton became an assembly area for the draftees of several counties, and the Chamber of Commerce urged everyone to give the soldiers a rousing send-off; local girls gathered at the railroad depots to cheer the soldiers.

In October of 1918 as victory seemed imminent the city's population fluctuated between euphoria and depression as it looked forward to victory on one hand and fought the dreadful flu epidemic that hit the nation on the other. On October 16, 1918 there were 94 cases of flu reported in Stockton. Four deaths were reported the next day and within a week there were 1,170 cases in the city. An ordinance was passed requiring everyone to wear a mask. The flu epidemic raged from mid-October 1918 until the first of February 1919. All segments of the community were affected, but perhaps none worse than the Orientals who could not get into the hospitals. As a result, the local Japanese Association built the Nippon Hospital in 1920 to care for family and friends. The hospital only operated for a couple of years before the Japanese population became too sparse to support it.

When news of the armistice arrived in Stockton shortly after midnight on November 11, whistles blew and bells rang throughout the city. People jumped from their beds and headed for the center of town to celebrate. A parade was held during the day (with many of the participants wearing flu masks). Public and private celebrations went on for 24 hours.

The city basked in pride over its contribution to victory. Newspapers throughout the country heaped on praise for the Caterpillar tank. The *Chicago Tribune* wrote, "no single mechanical invention in the great war did more in a mechanical way to bring victory than did the machine designed for the uses of peace. The plowing engine metamorphosis became the Juggernaut." Another credited the tank with saving 20,000 lives on the Somme in the fall of 1916.

By war's end the Holt Manufacturing plant had

been completely converted for the production of tanks. Now the company had half-completed equipment and no market, for it had neglected the farm tractor market throughout the war years. The Best Tractor Company, founded by the son of the Best Company owner Holt Manufacturing had previously bought out, dominated the farm market. Benjamin Holt died in December of 1920. Financial problems plagued the company as some short-term notes came due. Finally, out-of-town financiers who had backed the Best Company proposed a merger that resulted in the formation of the Caterpillar Tractor Company. This proved to be Stockton's loss as Best management gained control and moved company headquarters to Peoria, Illinois, in 1925 to be closer to their markets. That same year the Sperry Flour Mill moved its operations to Vallejo. Thus Stockton lost two major employers in one year. Historian Glenn Kennedy wrote about the move of the two companies:

For years and years the local populace condemned Holt and Sperry as being "sweatshops" paying "coolie" wages and made many other undue assertions. They thought the town would be better off without them. The loyal workers of the two companies know better. At one time Holt had 4,000 employees. When both moved away, the local "wise-guys" woke up to realize how wrong they were. Stockton had lost something they could never have again.

In 1919 Santa Clara's College of the Pacific, the oldest private college in the state, began looking for a new home. Rumors were flying that the college would come to Stockton. By the end of the year two

sites were offered and the school's trustees came to look them over. The school settled on a part of the Smith Tract, 40 acres of land traditionally used by the Italian gardeners. Classes were held in the Stockton Record Building with 40 students enrolled, as ground was broken in 1923. By 1924 there were nine buildings on the campus and by 1925, 605 students. The college has made a valuable contribution to the city's educational network.

During the World War I years building had slowed down; however, it was revitalized as Stockton entered a period of new growth and civic pride following the war. A city-wide reform movement was initiated, including a new zoning system developed to control the city growth. A new city charter, approved in 1922, provided for a city manager and that same year voters approved a million-dollar bond issue for public buildings. The city passed an ordinance outlawing the selling of farm products on city streets. The ordinance put the Italian Gardeners out of business overnight. Immediately the group appointed a committee to find a solution to its problem. The group organized the San Joaquin Marketing Association, but found that the Italian Gardener Society, being a non-profit corporation, could not own the association. Shares were sold and the group's leaders approached the

Machines always fascinated Ben Holt, as this photo attests. Here Holt (center) learns to master a flying machine after World War I, just prior to his death in 1920. Courtesy, Pacific Center for Western Historical Studies, University of the Pacific

Bank of Italy for financial support. According to local historian Tillio Boggiano, the bank's founder, Amadeo P. Giannini, said, "if it is for the farmers, yes!" They were granted the loan and built the association headquarters, known as Growers' Market, on the east side of Wilson Way near Weber Avenue. The growers continued to struggle until one of their members, Victorio Antonini, commenced hauling produce to San Francisco by truck. Soon Nathaniel A. Gotelli began trucking produce to Los Angeles and others followed. Thus the truck farmers of Stockton became major suppliers to two of California's largest cities.

The new city manager type of government went into effect in July 1923. Charles Ashburner was appointed city manager at a salary of $20,000 a year. He went to work immediately on city improvement projects, and received credit for the passing of another enormous bond issue in 1924. This issue included $1,500,000 for flood control—a dam on the upper Calaveras River at last! There was money for the Miner Avenue Subway, city parks, a new fire alarm system, street improvements, and new motor equipment.

Newly elected city officials enjoyed a honeymoon with the local populace. Local historian Glenn Kennedy wrote in 1967 of the usual treatment of politicians by Stockton's citizens:

Amusing as it may seem, each time new commissioners or councilmen were elected on election day they were the best that had ever been chosen. Six months later they were branded as not being any better than the last ones and it will probably be that way for as many years as the city elects new city fathers.

How true this was, for before long they nicknamed the new city manager "Cashburner," and the Miner Avenue Subway "Cashburner's Squirrel Hotel."

But those who wished to continue the improvement program pressed on. The Civic Memorial Auditorium was dedicated to the Stockton war dead in 1925, and the City Hall was added to the new Civic Center in 1927. More than nine square miles had been annexed to the city with the inclusion of residential areas as far north as the Calaveras River. Industrial development continued, and the Chamber of Commerce report recommended that the city encourage agricultural business.

In 1928 the population of Stockton was 56,000. There were 190 industries, employing 5,750 with an annual payroll of seven and a half million dollars. The value of industrial production was $38,000,000; the value of the previous year's county agricultural production was an impressive $52,000,000. The Stockton Chamber of Commerce Executive H.R. "Bob" Robertson coined the phrase "1,000 miles of waterways," as the city began to look back to its port to bring continued prosperity.

The roaring twenties had indeed been energetic years for Stockton, and the city looked forward to continued growth in the decade to come.

VI.

DEPRESSION, WAR, AND AFTERMATH

Stockton's economy remained healthy throughout the 1920s, up to and including 1929, despite ominous fluctuations in the stock market. After peaking in September the market plunged into a period of decline, followed by intermittent rallies until October when the crash toppled the nation's economy. Curiously, it is almost impossible to determine the actual date of the crash, or measure its national impact, by perusing local newspapers of the day, for business, at least in Stockton, went on as usual. The local economy received a boost when over two million dollars in privately funded building projects were pledged that year. Most important to the economic health of the city, however, was the deepening of Stockton Channel and the construction of the new port facilities, which were started in 1930.

The Calaveras flood control dam was completed in September of that year. Constructed as a shock absorber to take the pressure off Mormon Slough and the Calaveras River during periods of heavy storms, the dam promised to keep Stockton and the surrounding area from flooding. A dedication ceremony was held on November 2, 1930, during which City Manager Walter B. Hogan was praised for his efforts on behalf of the project.

On a cold, clear February morning in 1933, the S.S. *Daisy Gray,* the first ocean vessel to sail up the new deep-water channel, arrived in the Port of Stockton. Whistles blew and church bells rang, just as in the old days when a steamship would unexpectedly arrive in port. Approximately 1,000 people rushed to the dock to see the historical event. The ship, which carried 7,000 board feet of lumber, was efficiently

unloaded as spectators watched from the dock. A formal celebration was held in the Civic Auditorium on April 5, 1933. The town welcomed special guests including California's governor, James Rolph, Jr.

The celebration marked the end of the long struggle that culminated in the completion of the dam project. The town had taken the first steps toward digging a channel to the sea in 1871, but the price tag proved too high to make the project a reality. In 1906 the Stockton Chamber of Commerce hosted the chairman of the National Rivers and Harbors Commission on a tour of the San Joaquin River to discuss the project again. He commented, "You ought to have 15 feet of water to the sea." That became the slogan until 1917 when, as ships became bigger, the slogan was changed to "17 feet to the sea." The Army Corps of Engineers held a local hearing and sent a report to Washington, D.C., in an attempt to get federal approval and funding for the project, but the First World War delayed all action. The Chamber of Commerce did not give up. It requested another hearing on the project, and in June 1919 a local delegation went to Washington and came home with authorization for a complete survey and cost estimate. After another local hearing, in which the Board of Engineers for Rivers and Harbors vetoed the project, the Chamber once again requested a hearing in Washington. It was August of 1924 before they brought home a recommendation to undertake the project. The following year city voters approved a $1,307,500 bond issue for the city's share of the project by a margin of 13 to 1. By January of 1926 both the House and Senate had approved the project

At the peak of the 1920s the city economy was thriving. Members of the Chamber of Commerce took an excursion on the J.D. Peters *to appreciate the wealth generated from the delta farms along the 1,000-mile long waterway. By then the 880-ton vessel had stopped its routine overnight run to San Francisco and was used only for excursion trips. Courtesy, Stockton Chamber of Commerce*

As automobiles became a common sight all over town, accidents unfortunately increased. The collision between these two cars on the corner of El Dorado and | *Harding Way was nearly fatal to one of the drivers. Courtesy, Pacific Center for Western Historical Studies, University of the Pacific*

and included it in a federal bill which President Calvin Coolidge signed on January 21, 1927. By this time the designated depth was at 26 feet. The right of way, land for the port, and land on which to deposit the excess dredged material was acquired. Work started in 1930 and three years later the *Daisy Gray* sailed into port.

In 1932 city voters approved a plan to establish a port district and Col. Benjamin Casey Allin, a former Houston port director, was hired to take charge of operations. The port authority, with the assistance of the Chamber of Commerce, convinced the Interstate Commerce Commission to approve the construction of a belt line railroad system that would offer equal access to the town's three transcontinental railroads. The Southern Pacific, the Santa Fe, and the Western Pacific railroads agreed to take turns operating the road. Before the channel project was completed another application was sent to Washington to deepen the channel to 30 feet. Approval came in 1935 and the second dredging was completed by 1940.

The port building project had a strong influence on the city's economic well-being, even though it did not show a profit until 1936-1937. Historian Nicholas P. Hardman estimated that the project, which employed over 500 workers, cut the local unemployment rate by 20 to 25 percent.

Stockton's middle class did not fare badly during the Depression years, although there were changes in the lifestyles of its citizens; courtships lasted longer as couples delayed marriages for lack of money to set up housekeeping. Stockton families who needed money could always earn a little extra in nearby farmers' fields, and women went to work in the drying yards, packing sheds, and canneries.

One area of Stockton that grew rapidly during the Depression years was the west end, called Skid Road. (The term was later corrupted to Skid Row.) It was the oldest part of town, encompassing Chinatown and the area west of El Dorado Street. Before the automobile became commonplace most farm workers had been housed on the farms, and came to town only when they were between jobs or to buy necessities. The old buildings of the west end had

Downtown Stockton boasted many restaurants and lunch counters where a good meal could be had for as little as 35 cents. The Park Restaurant, shown in this 1935 photograph, was later known as the P. K. Lunch, and had an international staff of waitresses, cooks, waiters, and | *dishwashers. Also in the Main Street area was the Hart's Cafeteria and the Coney Island Chili Parlor, the local gathering place for the Greek colony in the 1920s. Courtesy, Pacific Center for Western Historical Studies, University of the Pacific*

The Wool Grower's Hotel stands as one of the many places various ethnic groups sought for a sense of nativity. Built in the 1880s, the hotel served as the early center for Basque gatherings and feasts.

Other citizens of the city treated themselves to the distinctive and tempting Basque food available there. Courtesy, Stockton Chamber of Commerce

traditionally served as rooming houses for these seasonal workers. During the late 1920s and early 1930s Filipinos comprised the major farm labor force on the delta. The men gathered in town on weekends after a week of labor in the fields. Many of these men had gone from the Philippines to work in the fields of Hawaii and had come to the mainland looking for work when their contracts expired. Since the Phillipine Islands were under U.S. jurisdiction there were no quotas on immigration. Some of the Filipinos worked in the Imperial Valley in the winter and Stockton in the summer. Filipino-run businesses were opened to meet their needs and part of Stockton's west end was given a new nickname, "Little Manila."

The Filipinos were welcomed in the west end but not in other parts of the city, for some downtown hotels even posted signs that read, "No Filipinos." Eventually the city would have the highest Filipino population in the U.S. A second wave of Filipinos arrived after World War II. Many were former servicemen, more educated than the first group, and perhaps faced less prejudice because of this.

The Depression brought a large influx of migrants looking for jobs. Stockton's reputation for providing

Women moved into cannery positions as soon as the plants were opened. Adept and skillful, these women proved to be the essential unit behind the success of many local canneries. Here women are seen processing and canning asparagus at the Flotill Cannery. Courtesy, Stockton Chamber of Commerce

The Great Depression brought another and more lasting problem to the city, the need for low-cost housing, which unfortunately created the climate for urban blight. Throughout the city's history its administrators had enforced strict building codes, but during the 1930s county officials allowed and encouraged subdivision with a minimum of required improvements. Often a graded street was all that was needed to start a development, and substandard housing on the edge of the city flourished.

Although Stockton's farmers did not go hungry they did not escape the Depression unscathed. They had difficulty paying their bills and in turn Stockton businesses suffered. The business community had always suffered periodic declines by extending credit to local farmers. The farmer had to wait until his crops were harvested to be paid, and expected the businessman to do the same. When agriculture shut down during the winter months, so did the business economy in town. But by 1940 the area had weathered the worst of the Depression and economic

Stockton canning industries prepared for the heavy war demands as this Flotill cannery poster incited both patriotism and independence in women. It was one of the rare industries which guaranteed women a job after the war. Courtesy, Stockton Public Library

farm jobs turned Skid Row into one street-long hiring hall. Displaced farmers of the Midwest and the dust bowl were attracted to Stockton's farm jobs, especially in the disastrous year of 1934. They came from Oklahoma, Arkansas, Missouri, and Texas. Many settled in East Stockton, which soon became known as "Okieville." Most were farmers but a few opened small businesses.

Many of the city's laborers found employment through the W.P.A. (Works Progress Administration), which had come to the city and taken on various public building projects. Most young men were able to find jobs, for a strong back seemed to be the major criteria for employment at the time. But as the Depression deepened those over 40 had great difficulty finding jobs, and for those over 50 it was almost impossible.

prospects looked hopeful as the minimum wage went to 50 cents per hour for men and 37.5 cents per hour for women. As war hovered over Europe, lightning struck out of the west. On December 7, 1941, the Japanese attacked Pearl Harbor and every person in the city of Stockton would find his life changed. The following day San Francisco radio stations went off the air as that city, along with Los Angeles and Sacramento, underwent blackouts because of a report that enemy aircraft were within 21 miles of the California coast. On December 9 aircraft were again reported, this time just 10 miles off the coast, and Stockton too considered blackouts, although they never came to pass.

The disaster at Pearl Harbor took its toll among local Japanese as old animosities surfaced. Air raid warnings and radio blackouts frayed nerves as rumors spread that the Japanese intended to invade and occupy California to take the farmland they coveted. Talk of internment of the Japanese population increased as a belief spread that there were spies in the Japanese community whose purpose was to aid in the invasion. Sheer hysteria led to wild rumors that flew about the countryside. There were so-called

"strange lights" supposedly sending signals from prime targets in California, and there were reports of unusual ground signs sighted from the air.

All Japanese were now branded as "Japs" by most of the local populace, even the Nisei (those born in the United States). By spring the federal government ordered all Japanese to relocation centers. Families sold their belongings for next to nothing or packed them into boxes and stored them in any convenient location. Some used barns for storage or boarded up houses, which were soon looted.

The War Relocation Authority leased the county fairgrounds as a holding center for the local Japanese. The fairgrounds' horse stables were converted into dormitories. By May 1942, there were 490 Stockton High School students at the camp. High school teacher Elizabeth Humbarger, sponsor for the school's

A 1944 day-care center was three decades ahead of the licensed nurseries prevalent in the late 1970s. Following through with their ads attracting female workers that guaranteed continual

employment after the war, Flotill Canneries also relieved working mothers' worries by providing a child care nursery on the cannery grounds. Courtesy, Stockton Public Library

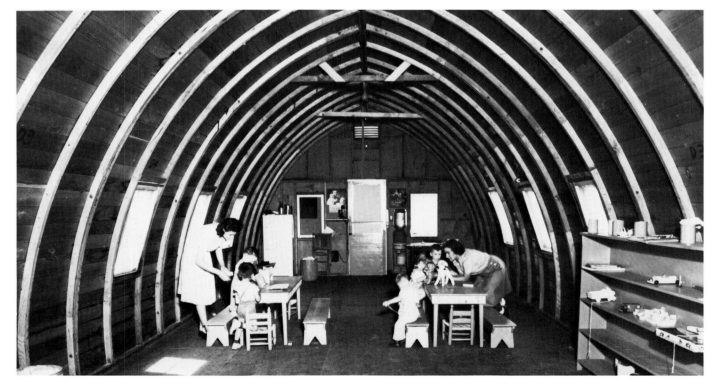

Left: During the war years Stockton boat builders numbered eight companies operating 10 shipyards with 10,000 workers. Among the large shipbuilders were Colberg, Stephen Brothers, Hickenbotham, and Pollick Shipyard, which was the largest, employing about 5,000 people. Here the Colberg Boat Works launches the USS ATR 52. Courtesy, Stockton Chamber of Commerce

Above: This photograph features a view of the Stockton Channel in the late 1930s, prior to the building of the Stockton grain elevators. Large ocean vessels found their way into the 26-foot-deep Stockton Channel as early as 1933 and by 1940 the channel was deepened to 30 feet. Clearly visible in the waterway is the turning basin. Courtesy, Stockton Chamber of Commerce

Japanese American Club, got permission to hold class at the camp for two hours per day. Acting as liaison, Humbarger asked the other teachers to send assignments to the students, enabling them to complete their school year. Most agreed. Humbarger organized the temporary school, enlisting college students to supervise the high school students. The plan worked; 92% of the students completed the year's work, and all of the senior class students graduated.

In October 1942 all of the local Japanese, including the Nisei, were sent to Rohor, Arkansas. Many of the young Nisei enlisted in the armed forces and served honorably during the war. In retrospect it is evident that a great injustice was done, the result of 50 years of prejudice and newspaper criticism of the Japanese in California. One might wonder if the city of Stockton, tolerant of foreign populations in the past, might have been so again had it not been for the spreading panic among the coastal cities.

During World War I, Stockton's Holt Manufacturing had made a significant contribution to the war effort with its tanks. But during World War II the manufacturing sector of the entire city launched into wartime production. In the shipyards alone the industrial work force grew from 2,500 in 1939 to 10,000 at the height of the war. Eight companies operated ten yards which built floating dry-dock sections, net tenders, rescue boats, submarine patrol boats, landing craft, transport ships, and small craft. Stockton companies received government contracts because they met the War Department's requirement that manufacturing of strategic military materiel be produced 60 miles or more from the sea in order to be outside the range of naval gunfire.

During the war years everything from aerial bombs and airplane parts to the reconditioning of army trucks and motors occupied the civilian work force, but it was the military installations that really changed the city. Most of the Port of Stockton, along with additional acreage, became the Stockton subdepot of the Benicia Arsenal, and was under army jurisdiction. Rough and Ready Island became the Naval Supply Annex, where the navy built the world's largest continuous concrete wharf to berth 13 ships in a single line. The army facility at Lathrop added to the city's store of military supplies and Stockton became the supply base of the Pacific. The local airport became an Air Force flight training school known as Stockton Field. It is no wonder that by the end of the war Stockton was considered the number one military target in California in case of enemy attack.

The city's population swelled during the war years, and emergency housing and military barracks were thrown up in and around the city. Downtown Stockton was bursting at the seams and the adjacent Skid Row grew.

During the World War II era another large

This picture of the southwest corner of California and Main streets depicts women during World War II. A U.S. Marine Corps recruitment poster on the sidewalk encourages women to enlist, while the WAC waiting at the corner is an example of the great number of women who did answer the call to serve their country. Courtesy, Pacific Center for Western Historical Studies, University of the Pacific

minority group appeared on the Stockton scene. There had long been a stable black community in Stockton, for some had come during the Gold Rush. There were black churches very early in Stockton's history and a black school had been established during the Civil War. After the children were integrated into the public school system there is little record of change in the black community, until the Second World War. Black military personnel were stationed in Stockton and the war brides of these servicemen followed. Others were attracted by the wartime industrialization of the area. Some of these new residents were Southern blacks with new-found freedom, who would never return to their former homes. Most settled in south Stockton in temporary government housing or in low-cost housing in the east part of town, some of which is still in use today. After the war some of the black servicemen returned to

Stockton to become part of the civilian government work force at the remaining military supply bases. The black community grew and suffered some discrimination, much of it caused by poor housing, leading to segregation in the schools. This created a new problem, which would have to be dealt with in later years.

Throughout the war years the area's agricultural sector suffered a severe labor shortage as former farm workers moved into wartime jobs. Field labor became scarce and fruit-pickers became almost nonexistent. High school students were encouraged to help harvest the crops and although schools were closed to facilitate their efforts some of the more perishable fruits were lost. Inmates from a German prisoner of war camp established at the fairgrounds also worked in the fields.

But these efforts to provide farm labor were not

An important military site during World War II, the Stockton Channel and the Stockton Naval Supply Depot on Rough and Ready Island (right) served as home for many naval ships after the war. This aerial view provides an excellent look at the ships of the Pacific Reserve Fleet tied up at the 6,500-foot-long continuous concrete wharf. Courtesy, Stockton Chamber of Commerce

Because of housing shortages during World War II, military barracks and emergency housing literally appeared overnight throughout the city. Building began with temporary trailers which within two months gave way to solidly constructed housing units. River View, southeast of the Port of Stockton, was constructed at the same time as Edison Villa and Parkside. Courtesy, Pacific Center for Western Historical Studies, University of the Pacific

The first Bracero Program was instituted when the city fathers welcomed the arrival of Mexican nationals on June 18, 1943. For more than 20 years the program provided the work force in the San Joaquin area needed to sustain the tomato and asparagus industries. Courtesy, Stockton Public Library

enough as farmers were urged to produce more for the war effort. There was still a need for a more abundant labor force, so the Bracero Program was initiated to answer the need. Braceros were Mexican laborers brought into the area to work on the farms and in the orchards. Special camps were established as trainloads of workers arrived from Mexico. The Braceros were willing workers, earning American dollars to take or send home, and there is no doubt that ,hey helped save California agriculture.

Although Mexican farm workers had been immigrating into the U.S. since the 1930s, few worked in the fields around Stockton, the exception being the sheep-shearers and livestock workers who had been part of Stockton's agricultural tradition since its early days. The Bracero program continued long after the war, and by 1964, when the program was finally shut down, more than half of the delta work force was made up of Mexicans. Many of these workers returned to Stockton under the new green card program or illegally entered the state to work in the fields, and Stockton's resident Mexican population grew.

After the war the military repair shops converted back to manufacturing farm machinery and trailers. Shipbuilders returned to making fishing boats, river barges, gold dredgers, luxury pleasure craft, and farm machinery. The Port of Stockton had been forced to neglect regular shipping during the war years, and found itself outside the mainstream of the shipping business. Bulk storage facilities for oil, iron ore, and liquids such as wine and molasses were added. New warehouses were constructed and became a major factor in the port's business. But increase in ship sizes and the depth limitation in the channel kept the port from competing with the coastal ports in the newly developing business of container shipping. Once again there was a move to deepen the channel, but once again it would take years to get through the red tape, and it would not be until the 1970s that the port began to show a healthy profit again.

Fortunately for the city the military bases did not shut down entirely. More than 6,000 civilian employees were hired at the Stockton Ordnance Depot, the Stockton General Depot (now Sharp's

Growth and permanence of the Sharpe General Depot at Lathrop added greatly to Stockton's population and economy. This picture shows dedication ceremonies of the Sharpe Army Airfield and features the John J. Pershing hangar in 1960. Courtesy, United States Army Photograph

Army Depot), and the Naval Depot, which became headquarters of the 19th U.S. Fleet.

Recovery from the pressures of a wartime economy was slow, but it did occur. Stockton now had time to turn to solving some of the city's problems. SUSD (Stockton Unified School District) was under great stress from the increase in population and school enrollment. Half-day sessions and overcrowded classrooms had unfortunately become the norm, so the school district instituted, in 1948, a so-called "6-4-4 system" to relieve the situation. The system allowed for six elementary grades, while the seventh through tenth grades were moved to the old Stockton High School on the corner of Harding Way and California streets. Grades 11 and 12 were included with the two years of Stockton College. The district had operated under the original grammar school/high school system for 82 years with no change until 1935, when the first junior college was organized, after two aborted attempts had been made in 1917 and 1921. The school district contracted with the College of the Pacific to operate Stockton Junior College under a rental agreement. The junior college facilities operated under this system until the new system was organized in 1948. The district renamed the facility Stockton College and moved to property just south of the Pacific campus.

After a series of successful bond issues and an expanded building program, SUSD changed the whole system again in 1952, this time to the 6-3-3 system, which allowed for six elementary grades, three junior high school grades, and three senior high school grades. There were now three high schools—Edison, Franklin, and the newly organized Stagg High School, which operated on the Stockton College campus until a new facility was opened in 1958.

In 1963 SUSD terminated the junior college program when San Joaquin Delta College was organized to serve a wider area than just Stockton. After considerable negotiations the new college district leased the old Stockton College campus and remained there until moving to the new campus on the former State Hospital Farm on Pacific Avenue.

Downtown Stockton encountered new problems in the postwar era brought on particularly by the increased number of automobiles. Parking became impossible and, giving in to frustration, people double-parked. The congestion caused frequent accidents; at times there seemed to be an accident at every corner. Skid Row continued to be the hiring hall for farm labor contractors who now found enough Mexican workers to meet their needs. Stockton had the dubious honor of having the largest Skid Row in the United States. The police department was factionalized, demoralized, and riddled with graft. Most of Stockton's police chiefs had been easy-going, good-natured men whose priorities were not discipline and efficiency.

In January of 1946 City Manager Walter Hogan appointed Rex Parker, a detective in the department, as chief of police, and gave him the task of shaping up the department. Parker, an energetic and apparently incorruptible man, set to work. He cleaned up the police station by making it a place of business instead of a local hangout for those who had nothing to do.

Some of the officers were reported to be on the take, accepting everything from a carton of cigarettes to large-denomination bills, so Parker decided to dry up the source of the money. Believing a local bookmaker to be the source of much of this graft money, he closed the business in March of 1946. He also made administrative changes and started training programs and a police reserve department.

In the spring of 1947 City Manager Hogan attended a conference on organized crime held by Governor Earl Warren. He returned home convinced that outside racketeers were moving into the old Stockton gambling community. He consulted with Parker, who immediately closed down the 16 wide-open gambling operations in town. Soon the Stockton employment office received applications and granted unemployment insurance checks to 400 self-professed professional gamblers.

Parker next went after the slot machine business and informed the owners of these devices that no money payoffs would be allowed, and that the machines could be used for amusement only. In taking these steps, Parker was stepping on previously untouched toes, for many of the local lodge halls used slot machine money to stay solvent. He also put the heat on local houses of prostitution, with the result that some of the girls left town or turned to working the local streets and bars.

In January of 1948 five new council members took office. One of them was a Skid Row businessman who would soon surface as the majority leader. Several months after taking office he invited the council members to his home for the evening. Most of them went, and admittedly, they discussed government business. The next day rumors spread that they would

ask Hogan to remove Parker from office. Some concerned citizens feared this meant that Stockton would go back to being an "open" town and made plans to resist the movement. But Mayor Jerry Keithley announced that the council would continue to support strict law enforcement. Things remained the same until August when Keithley resigned from the council to take a city job. A friend of the Skid Row businessman/councilman was appointed to the council in his place.

Before long the council pressured Hogan to investigate reports that Parker could not get along with his subordinates and implied that Hogan's job was at stake. Rumors spread again, and petitions were circulated by concerned citizens. One petition in support of Hogan and Parker contained 3,662 signatures. Another, carrying 80 policemen's signatures, declared there was a lack of confidence in Parker and a reluctance to serve under the chief.

The council could not fire Parker, but it could, and did, fire Hogan, and appointed his assistant Russell McGee as acting city manager. This was almost sacreligious in the minds of some, as Hogan had served the city faithfully for 28 years. A citizen's committee was organized. The Grand Jury met and recommended that Hogan be reinstated. When the council refused, the citizen group started collecting signatures for a recall of the six councilmen. The *Stockton Record* and a leading Stockton banker supported the recall. The opposition believed it could not get fair coverage in the newspaper. They retaliated by publishing their own newspaper, which was delivered to 25,000 citizens every ten days.

As the issues became more clearly defined, Stockton's citizens divided into two distinct camps. The pro-recallers were perceived by the opposition as rich, intellectual, and Protestant—all in the same group. This brought labor, the "common" man, and Italians, because most were Catholic, into the anti-recall camp. The business community tried to remain neutral, although there were some who believed an open town was good for business and others who had never forgiven Parker for closing down the slot machines at their clubs. The town's newer residents, who felt no particular loyalty to Hogan, leaned

toward the anti-recall movement. Others believed that since the policemen signed the petition against Chief Parker there must be some truth to the complaints about his leadership. Some members of the Stockton legal community muddied the waters further by offering unauthorized deals on both sides.

On election day 20,000 voters, more than in any previous election, turned out and defeated the recall by 1,200 votes. Local citizens shrugged their shoulders and went back to business as usual, but out-of-town newspapers headlined, "Stockton Voted An Open Town." One unbiased report was filed by Gordon Pate of the *San Francisco Chronicle*. He drew some interesting conclusions:

So far as opening the town goes, first, the Council is on record as opposing it, and second even if it wished to, it could not open the town at present. Too many people are watching, including the only newspaper in town.

The recallers had not really lost because the city never became wide open again. They had achieved their purpose. Hogan quietly retired but soon became a water consultant for the county, two water districts, and the Port of Stockton. After the new city councilmen took office the Calaveras Dam was renamed Hogan Dam in his honor. In 1959 he received special citations from the Army Corps of Engineers and the Secretary of the Army for his service in solving the area's water problems.

Despite the fact that the citizens of Stockton had become divided over the 1949 recall issue, there was one area of Stockton life that united everyone: that was football fever. Amos Alonzo Stagg, the Grand Old Man of Football from the University of Chicago, moved to the College of the Pacific well past retirement age for most men in the late 1930s and put together many winning teams. The Football Coaches'

Association awarded Stagg Coach of the Year honors in 1943. Stagg retired in 1946 and was replaced by coach Larry Semmering who put together another winner in 1949, the highest scoring team in the nation. The team played small colleges, so it did not receive national recognition, even though it scored a season total of 575 points. Semmering's team was undefeated and untied, yet uninvited to a bowl game. The team was headed by an unusually small quarter-back, Eddie Le Baron, a master ball-handler who became a professional football star.

The year 1949 also saw the metropolitan area extend its boundaries as the county planning commission allowed a new development in the virgin area north of Stockton. Long-time Stockton realtor Greenlaw Grupe broke ground for the residential development of Lincoln Village in 1949 and the Lincoln Village Shopping Center in 1951. The district's one-room schoolhouse became the seed of a major new district, the Lincoln Unified School District. Unlike some other county developers, Grupe provided residents with adequate water and sewer facilities. The area was annexed to the city by degrees between 1955 and 1969.

Stockton city limits moved north of the Calaveras River for the first time in 1952. Several more parcels of land were annexed in 1954 and 1955. Charles M. Weber III started the Weberstown residential development along Pacific Avenue in the latter year.

Other developers followed, and housing complexes sprung up north of the river like mushrooms in the fertile soil.

Following the growth of the residential area north of the river, shopping centers were the next natural step in development. Weber developed the Weberstown Mall, one of the first covered shopping centers in California. Unfortunately, shopping malls proved to be bad investments for many during the 1960s because of the large sums tied up in buildings and the slow return. Weber fared no better than many when he lost his investment, in spite of the fact that he attracted major department stores like Sears and Roebuck and Weinstocks.

As the city moved north, less attention was paid to the southern part of town. When it came time to build a new bridge over Mormon Slough city officials decided instead to install a large culvert. In December of 1955 six inches of rain fell in three days in Stockton and even more in the foothills to the east. The Diverting Canal could not hold the water, and it overflowed at the point where it connected to Mormon Slough; the latter once again became a river. The city was endangered as culverts restricted the water flow. Dynamite and draglines were used in an attempt to remove the obstructions in the slough but the water continued to rise. City officials decided to save downtown Stockton and threw up a sandbag dike on the north levee. South Stockton went under water. On Christmas Eve in 1955 more than 3,000 people were evacuated in the east and south edges of town. The city fathers had talked of the need for a new enlarged Hogan Dam on the Calaveras River, but nothing had been done. The citizens of South Stockton gathered 2,072 signatures on a petition which they presented to the council demanding action to prevent future flooding. By September 1956 plans for a new Hogan Dam were on the drawing boards. No doubt the flood had given impetus to the project. The new dam was completed in 1964.

Other city improvements followed. The question of a new courthouse arose in 1944 as county government offices had, by that time, spread out to five downtown locations and to a Hazelton Avenue complex. A newspaper editorial suggested that all

offices be situated in one building near the courthouse. The county decided not to abandon the old Court House Square but to demolish the courthouse and rebuild on the site. The county purchased the Hotel Stockton to be used as an interim courthouse while the new one was under construction.

The grand old building was razed and even though it had been condemned 30 years before, it took considerable effort on the part of the wrecking ball to bring it down. Ground for the new building was broken in 1961, and on October 10, 1964 dedication ceremonies were held. The zinc statue of Justice had been removed from the old courthouse dome and was placed at the west entrance to the building.

Center Street was extended across Stockton Slough and the extension of McLeod Lake east of Center Street was filled. The legal problems of filling Stockton Channel again proved problematical because of Weber's will. Charles M. Weber III proposed the construction of a ten-story office building with adequate parking, but the project was never begun. Weber and the city settled for providing parking space only; thus the parking lot sits on stilts today over the official head of navigation on Stockton Channel.

In 1962, after suffering three defeats, a library bond issue in the amount of $1,740,000 received voter approval and the city proceeded with plans for a new city facility in the Civic Center. The Stockton Library had come a long way from the two second-floor rooms it occupied in 1880. In 1884 it moved to the Masonic Temple. Frank Stewart's $5,000 legacy to the institution in 1889 enabled the city to build a two-story brick structure on a Weber-donated lot. Two years later Dr. W.P. Hazelton, a former Stockton resident, donated $75,000, which was used to construct a granite and marble structure fronted by marble Grecian columns. When the new library was built in the Civic Center the Grecian columns were moved to the College of the Pacific campus.

The two 1962 civic building projects—the courthouse and the library—cost more than all the civic improvement projects of the 1920s combined. In 1960 it was reported that one third of a billion dollars in building projects were in the planning stages for the city and ajdacent areas.

In the summer of 1960 the Chamber of Commerce organized Captain Weber Days, which grew into a ten-day sports spectacular. In 1964 the event was reported to have been attended by over 200,000 persons who enjoyed 29 major sports events from polo to autocross racing in downtown Stockton. The official celebration was discontinued in 1980, but some events are still held, with no sign of diminishing interest.

It is not surprising that Stockton has become a sports town, particularly when one looks at the community's long history of athletic activities. Much of the enthusiasm began with President Theodore Roosevelt's interest in physical fitness. In 1913 the schools allowed children a half day off to march through the streets of Stockton carrying banners asking for playgrounds. The pleas were answered the following year with the organization of a city play-ground commission. Bert Swenson became the

director of the department in 1918 and earned the title "Dean of Recreation" during his 36 years of service. He supervised the acquisition and construction of the municipal camp at Silver Lake in Amador County, municipal golf courses, tennis courts, swimming pools, and other playground facilities.

During 1944 the cooperation of the schools led to an expanded playground program, but it was 1954 that saw the biggest change — the organization of a new Metropolitan Parks and Recreation Commission.

By 1965 the city was booming. It had become a desirable place in which to live, with new homes, new schools, new highways, recreational opportunities, and jobs for most. From 1950 to 1965 more building and growth had occurred in the city than in the previous 100 years.

This view looking west from the head of the Stockton Channel depicts the Stockton of today. Courtesy, Richard S Minnick, Sr.

BY AUGUSTUS KOCH.

1 COURT HOUSE.
2 FEMALE INSANE ASYLUM.
3 MALE "
4 WASHINGTON SCHOOL.
5 LAFAYETTE "
6 FRANKLIN "
7 1ST BAPTIST CHURCH.
8 EPISCOPAL "
9 JEWISH SYNAGOGUE.
10 NORTH METHODIST CHURCH.
11 SOUTH " "
12 CUMBERLAND PRESB?."

13 CHRISTIAN CHURCH.
14 PRESBYTERIAN "
15 GERMAN "
16 R. CATHOLIC "
17 CONGREGATIONAL "
18 COLORED "
19 "
20 YOSEMITE HOTEL.
21 WEBER HOUSE.
22 LAFAYETTE "
23 GRANT HOTEL.
24 STOCTON "

STOCKTON IN 1852.

BIRDS EYE VIEW OF THE CITY OF
STOCKTON
SAN JOAQUIN COUNTY   1870.   CALIFORNIA.

This hand-colored lithograph, derived from the original painting by Augustus Koch, portrays a bustling, developing Stockton in the 1870s. Commercial boats and trains entering the town from the north and south took advantage of the inland port city. Courtesy, Amon Carter Museum

25 ODD FELLOW BUILD?
26 DRUIDS HALL.
27 THEATRE BUILD?
28 STOCKTON WATER WORKS.
29   "   GAS   "
30 R.R. PASSENGER DEPOT.
31   "   FREIGHT   "
32 STOCKTON LUMBER YARD.
33   "   CITY FLOUR MILLS.
34   "   LANES
35 EUREKA WARE HOUSE.
36 GLOBE IRON WORKS.

37 W? P. MILLERS CARRIAGE FACT?
38 CONDY BROS? SASH & BLIND FACTERY.
39 TURN HALL.
40 RACE TRACK.
41 M.L ABRAMSKY, REAL ESTATE AGENT.
42 ELDORADO BREWERY.
43 CITY BREWERY
44 STOCKTON IRON WORKS.
45 PACIFIC TANNERY.
46 YO SEMITE CLOTHING HOUSE

Left: This painting of a youthful Captain Charles M. Weber by local artist Oscar Galgiani hung in the north wing of the State Capitol for more than 30 years. It now adorns the council chamber in city hall. Galgiani painted Weber's face from an old daguerrotype, while the rest of the portrait contains symbols of Stockton and Weber's legacy. Courtesy, Richard S. Minnick, Sr.

Facing page, bottom left: This Greg Custodio mural in the foyer of city hall represents the community spirit of the early pioneers and the important contribution each made to the development of Stockton. Courtesy, Richard S. Minnick, Sr,

Facing page, bottom right: This brilliant seashell picture was one of many unusual promotional cards produced by the Holden Drug Store, which was founded in 1849 by Dr. Erastus S. Holden. His son Isaac sold the family business in 1892, and after several proprietors the store folded in the 1950s. Courtesy, M.A. Lawrence Collection

Greeting cards for special occasions became a fashionable method of advertising among many Stockton merchants. Rosenbaum and Crawford Clothiers sent this embossed Easter greeting to their many customers after the turn of the century. Collecting merchants' cards became a popular hobby during that time period. Courtesy, M.A. Lawrence Collection

Above: For 75 years this nine-room house belonging to the Karl Simon family graced the corner of Madison and Fremont streets. In 1980 the Lou Galli family bought the Queen Anne cottage and barged it through the deep-water channel around various riverbends to its new location north of Tracy. Courtesy, Betty Galli

Left: A hand-carved lion's head on a cherrywood mantle is one example of the elegance in Victorian homes. This mantle was made in 1895 for Karl and Louise Simon's house. Courtesy, Betty Galli

The Pioneer Room at the Haggin Museum contains an outstanding artifact collection that carefully documents Stockton's history. Courtesy, Haggin Museum

Above: The College of the Pacific changed its name to the University of the Pacific in 1960. Through the main gate is a view of Burns Tower, built in 1963. Named for its late president, Robert Burns, the tower houses administrative offices and a water tank. Photo by Bela Fischer

Left: The 165-acre San Joaquin Delta College campus is situated on the former State Hospital farm grounds. Located in the heart of town, the graceful setting of the two-year college lends itself to a blend of the Mother Lode influence and the Spanish mission era in California. Photo by Bela Fischer

Visitors take an antique truck ride through the park at the Annual Spring Time on the Farm held at the San Joaquin Historical Museum. The museum located in Micke Grove Park is operated by the San Joaquin County Historical Society under a contractual agreement with the elected County Supervisors.

Above: Beautification of the downtown area in the 1960s included the closing of Main Street at Hunter Square and the creation of a fountain-centered plaza west of the San Joaquin County Court House. Courtesy, Stockton Chamber of Commerce

Right: This golden California bear guards the pillared Stockton Memorial Civic Auditorium. The cornerstone for the building was laid in November 1924, and the following year on Armistice Day, veteran units dedicated the 5,000-seat structure to Stockton's fallen sons. Photo by Bela Fischer

Left: A clear day and graceful trees surrounding sparkling water add beauty to a canoe outing in a local Stockton residential area. Photo by Bela Fischer

Facing page, bottom: Stocktonians' love for the delta waterway and the joy of living on waterfront property have inspired housing developers to build man-made lakes and inlets as part of the special features in their subdivisions. This intricate canal system in a modern apartment complex serves as an aesthetic urban version of the delta waterway. Courtesy, Stockton Chamber of Commerce

Below: Mammoth ocean-going vessels laden with cargo sail through the heavily-traveled deep-water channel. Sailing enthusiasts enjoy working their way up the Stockton Channel and look forward to participating in the many boat parades and regattas scheduled throughout the year. Courtesy, Stockton Chamber of Commerce

Above: A young man sells a bag of peaches at the Farmers Market held each Friday on Main Street in downtown Stockton. Downtown office workers utilize their lunch hour to purchase fresh fruit for the weekend. The market is sponsored by the Stockton Downtown Alliance.

Left: Founded by Italian immigrant Manlio Silva in 1926 and led by the celebrated Korean maestro Kyung-Soo Won for the past 17 seasons, the Stockton Symphony represents the pinnacle of Stockton's cultural influence. Historically, the symphony is the fifth-oldest continuous service orchestra in California. Courtesy, Steve Pereira

Above: A crowd of spectators witnessed the Majestic Explorer *on her maiden voyage at the Stockton Yacht Club. Photo by Bela Fischer*

Right: Sails filling with gentle wind, this sailboat leaves the head of the Stockton Channel, gliding past Stockton in the early morning light. Courtesy, Stockton Chamber of Commerce

The San Francisco 49er
players take the field at a
controlled practice held
with the San Diego
Chargers in Stockton in
August 1998. Amos
Alonzo Stagg Stadium
at the University of
Pacific overflowed with
28,000 fans at the
preseason event.

VII.

THE METROPOLIS

Stockton changed from a settled community to a rapidly sprawling metropolis during the 1950s, bringing new urbanization problems and unrest to the 1960s and early 1970s—another pivotal period in the city's history.

As suburbs developed under county control around the city, community leaders became absorbed in the problems of decay in the 100-year-old inner city. In 1955 Mayor Dean De Carli appointed an Urban Blight Committee to study the city's problems. The first urban renewal project was undertaken in east Stockton in the vicinity of Myrtle Street and Highway 99. This was a slum area which had been originally developed under the county government in the late 1800s and which had deteriorated badly during the Great Depression. Wood and tarpaper shacks had grown like toadstools from lots as small as 25 by 50 feet. The district was cleared and rebuilding was begun. Low-income housing projects were developed under city regulations on a portion of the land. Two new schools, a steel company, and other building projects renewed the area. Room was saved for a highway interchange and for a crosstown freeway to connect with the proposed Westside Freeway (today's I-5). This same crosstown connection was still far from completion by the early 1980s.

In 1958 the city council organized the West-end Redevelopment Project, which proved to be a political football. The major conflict occurred over whether to completely or partially demolish a nine-block area containing 162 rundown buildings and 48 bars. This was the very heart of Stockton's infamous Skid Row. After much heated discussion and two votes by the city council the resolution to demolish the whole area was passed. Criticism was levied at the council by those opposing demolition but the council held steadfast. Condemnation proceedings on a few of the properties delayed the project until 1964. The following year the west end took on the appearance of a war zone as the wrecker's ball leveled block after block of Skid Row. Only three buildings were left in the nine-block area, the old Eureka Grain or Farmers Union Warehouse, the Nippon Hospital, and the Sperry Flour office.

The two major ethnic groups that had been strongly entrenched in Skid Row were given priority to rebuild. The Lee Family Association built on the south side of the old Chinatown block and other Chinese associations and individuals filled the remainder. Filipino community leaders replaced "Little Manila" with a block of retail stores, offices, and a high-rise apartment building. El Dorado Street became banker's row and Center Street on both sides of the channel became the site of two modern motels.

The downtown shopping district continued to deteriorate as shopping centers were developed close to the new bedroom communities in north Stockton. Early in the 1960s an attempt was made to improve the business district as new facades were constructed on existing buildings and one-way streets were established to improve traffic flow. The buildings on the west side of Hunter Square were refurbished and an extensive beautification project was undertaken. A mall was created by closing off the west end of Main Street and a striking new fountain was added to embellish the area. Throughout the downtown area

Nightfall adds beauty and dramatic effects to the Hilton Hotel and the grand canal at the Venetian Bridges shopping area. Photo by Bela Fischer

By closing off the west end of Main Street and adding a fountain, the Hunter Square Plaza no longer reminds oldtimers of the fairs and expositions held at that location in the past. However, historic buildings such as the Bank of Stockton, California Building, Grupe Building, and the Fox California Theater stand as solid remembrances of the city long ago. Courtesy, Sylvia Sun Minnick

old buildings were condemned to make way for parking lots. But every time this was done more businesses closed, thus giving the general public fewer and fewer reasons to fight traffic to get to downtown establishments. To complicate matters even more, the demolishing of Skid Row left a void in low-income housing for the farm workers, indigent, and elderly, many of whom moved into the now aging and deteriorating downtown hotels.

The late 1960s were turbulent years for Stockton, as they were for many other cities. The first and only successful recall of a city councilman occurred in 1967. The previous year the city council had organized a charter revision committee to explore the possibilities of a mayoral system, and the public became uneasy. A city planning commissioner resigned in protest, accusing Councilman/Mayor James Rishwain of interference in a zoning matter. Next the city fired a deputy city manager and a citizen's group rose in protest, threatening to recall the full city council. By the following spring opposition to the mayoral system had swelled when the results of a private survey among local service clubs revealed there was an overwhelming desire to retain the city manager type of government. The matter was finally settled at the polls when Rishwain was recalled by a two-to-one vote. The local newspaper tried to calm the troubled waters.

The next major political issue arose in 1968 when minorities protested the method used to elect the city council. The city was divided into nine districts with a requirement that one councilman must reside in each district; however, the voting for each was held city-wide. When an individual representing a south Stockton district won an election but did not carry his own district, the district voters protested vehemently and the general population agreed. In November

1969, the city council voted 6-3 to put district voting on the ballot. The general public confirmed the decision and the system was changed to district voting, allowing only those in each district to vote for their representative.

In 1969 the city council was seeking a strong city manager who could deal with the politics and the urbanization problems of Stockton. They found the man they were looking for in Elder Gunter, a man described by many as a first-rate problem-solver. He brought with him 25 years of civic experience, including the management of six cities. Gunter faced major problems immediately. Perhaps the most serious was a cease-and-desist order clamped on the city by the state to prevent further industrial development because of inadequate sewer facilities. This was aimed directly at the food processing industry, which produced a huge volume of sewage during the peak of the canning season. And, there were other problems such as complaints of police brutality which culminated in a riot at an Oak Park rock concert on April 29, 1973. Urban renewal issues also loomed large. As the new city manager and city

There was still much open field between the Weberstown subdivision (left) and the Sherwood Manor estates (right) in the early 1960s. The field eventually became two shopping malls 10 years later.

The State Hospital farm complex on Pacific Avenue (center) was to give way to the modern campus of San Joaquin Delta College in 1972. Courtesy, Stockton Development Center

council faced inner city problems, there was an even larger problem to be dealt with by the SUSD (Stockton Unified School District) in solving the problem of school integration.

As Stockton moved north so did the city's affluent, which left the low-income population and minorities in south and east Stockton. Edison High School in the south end of town had a large percentage of minorities, principally blacks, Hispanics, and Orientals. Franklin High School on the east side of town had the most balanced racial mixture but it was predominantly low income. The major racial conflicts occurred on this campus. Stagg High School in the north became almost all white, analogous to the already white Lincoln Unified School District further

107

north. A busing plan was proposed by an integration committee, but strong opposition arose, delaying action. Minority groups protested integration delays and another class struggle took place in the city. Court action finally forced busing on the Stockton Unified School District. The district lost enrollment because of "white flight" into the north suburbs, which swelled enrollment in the Lincoln Unified School District. SUSD officials predicted a two-million-dollar deficit in 1972. The city grew so far north it stretched into the Lodi Unified School District, another predominantly white school system. The north end did not stay all white, however, as federal funds provided for some low-income housing and developers built many multiple-housing units to fill the area's need.

Morris Chapel was built in 1942 on the University of the Pacific grounds, and houses the Methodist Archives. Ivy gracing the exterior walls of the chapel, coupled with the rose bridal path, proved to be the favorite location for many students, alumni, and local citizens' weddings. Courtesy, Pacific Center for Western Historical Studies, University of the Pacific

By 1982 SUSD enrollment had started to rise again and predictions are that the trend will continue. The district continued to have financial and management problems, and in both 1981 and 1982 grand juries recommended that the school trustees resign and be replaced.

The northward population growth can also be attributed in part to the expansion of both the community college and the university. San Joaquin

Delta College moved to a new campus in 1972. After a long struggle over site selection, the district purchased the old State Hospital Farm on Pacific Avenue. Old buildings and a large number of mature trees occupied the site. The buildings were demolished but the trees were saved. A modern campus was constructed in an old environment, creating a unique setting. Today the college serves not only San Joaquin County but some areas of surrounding counties as well.

The College of the Pacific became known as the University of the Pacific in 1960, with the former becoming a liberal arts college within the university. The university consists of a number of colleges offering studies in liberal arts, music, engineering, education, pharmacy, and business/public administration. It offers off-campus study in foreign countries, the McGeorge School of Law in Sacramento, and the School of Dentistry in San Francisco. The university, which is a chartered Methodist college, is privately funded and is the oldest private institution on the West Coast. It adds considerably to the cultural richness and the economic health of the city of Stockton.

The new residential area in north Stockton moved west into the delta as Fritz Grupe, son of the Lincoln Village developer, built a planned community of mixed housing. This is Lincoln Village West, situated between Fourteen Mile and Five Mile Sloughs on land below sea level. Grupe took advantage of this unique situation, constructed a man-made lake and built homes, apartments, and condominiums on the shore. The company won national awards for its development, but Stockton reaped the most benefit because it led to a new trend in the city and focused attention on the water at the city's doorstep. Grupe continued to develop lakeside communities and other developers took up the waterfront theme.

Urban sprawl had long exceeded the bounds of Capt. Charles M. Weber's well-planned city of ample streets. Getting across town became more and more difficult with only two main north-south arteries, El Dorado and Pacific avenues, to carry the north-south flow of traffic. Construction in the north end of the city was spurred on with the completion of I-5 (Inter-

state Highway 5) through the city. Final completion of the last 15 miles of highway between Stockton and Sacramento took longer than planned because of the attitude of Governor Jerry Brown's administration toward building freeways. But the opening of the final leg of the freeway probably did more to improve the city's image than any other event in its history. There had always been beautiful homes on tree-shaded streets in town but travelers never saw them. They saw instead the slums along Highway 99 and the old rundown areas in south Stockton. At one time the famous Lincoln Highway cut right through the heart of Skid Row. For these reasons the city was considered a dirty town by many. When the I-5 bridge was constructed across Stockton Channel travelers were treated to a panoramic view of the city, including an impressive overview of the port.

The Port of Stockton experienced major problems during the early 1970s. A series of port directors were hired and fired, commissioners squabbled, and the facility lost money for seven years. There was talk of closing the operation down. A grand jury commissioned a study and action was taken to remedy the situation. The port commissioners hired a dynamic new port director, Alexander Krygsman. Krygsman managed to turn the situation around. Ships were still growing in size and the channel needed deepening again. The project had been approved in 1965 but was stalled in the red tape of environmental issues. Krygsman went to work and the project was reactivated. The Army Corps of Engineers let the contract in September of 1982 and dredging was begun in 1983. This time the goal was 38 feet to the sea.

In the 1850s Stockton's water table had been as high as 35 feet from the surface. Deep artesian wells were drilled and the excess water ran into the nearby sloughs. Householders did not look to the city to take care of their water needs as each had his own shallow well, water tank, and windmill. In Stockton, everyone was more concerned with excess water than the lack of it. City officials had been amused observers when, in the early 1900s, farmers from the Calaveras River and the Mormon Slough fought each other for irrigation water in the Linden/Bellota area

A 1,081-ton building module is shown here being moved from its construction site to a barge on the waterfront, its destination Prudhoe Bay on the north slope of Alaska. These modules, built in Stockton in 1983, are a part of the "waterflood system" to increase oil recovery while the "wellpad manifold system" is to maximize the use of SOHIO's 150 miles of crude oil flowlines. Courtesy, Richard S. Minnick

in eastern San Joaquin County. The San Joaquin East Water District (now Stockton East Water District) was organized to settle that battle but it was years before the city became concerned with the supply of drinking water. It was in the 1970s, when saline water began to show up in the wells on the west edge of the city, that concern began to grow. The city joined the San Joaquin East Water District and took up the fight for completion of the proposed Folsom South Canal down the east side of the Great Valley to bring American River water to the area.

Stockton's reliance on deep-water wells became critical as both urban and agricultural areas drew more and more water from under ground. The water table dropped dramatically and brackish water continued to intrude on the freshwater pool under Stockton. The water district joined with the city to pipe water from the Calaveras River at Bellota to a new water treatment plant on the east side of town in 1976. In spite of this, water conservation measures were necessary to maintain the water supply during the drought of the late 1970s. The Calaveras River, unlike many of the rivers that flow out of the Sierra Nevada range, does not drain a snow area thus providing a year-round water flow; it has only rainwater runoff, which cuts down the water quality. The city applied for delta water, even though it was of questionable quality, but dropped the application in 1984 as the Stockton East Water District signed a contract for New Melones water from the Stanislaus watershed.

As the city tried to find solutions to its water problems, a rapidly expanding population created urban sprawl. By 1980 the population within the city limits had reached 149,779; another 55,610 residents living adjacent to the city limits increased the Stockton metropolitan population to 205,389. In 1983 the city population showed an increase of 17,912, raising the total number of metropolitan residents to over 220,000. Although there is some duplication of city/county services, city services are often strained by the burden of additional county residents. This condition continues to cause conflicting interests between city and county governing bodies.

The population continues to grow as new immigrants arrive in Stockton. It is now the Southeast Asians, Vietnamese, Laotians, and Cambodians who are struggling to make their place in the community. Despite efforts by some to stop the influx of refugees, Stockton will no doubt, as it has in the past, accept these minorities into the mainstream of the community.

Because the mechanization of agriculture has reduced farm labor needs, there is a need for more industrial jobs to provide employment for these new immigrants. It took the city eight years to solve the sewer problem that hampered the development of new industrial plants. A new sewer facility costing over $16,000,000 was installed in 1979, but industrial development does not come easily. A major waterfront industrial project created controversy in 1981 as land across the channel from the port was proposed for the site of a Sohio (Standard Oil of Ohio) project to consist of modular building units to house pumping facilities for the Prudhoe Bay Alaskan oilfields. The question was whether there should be industrial or residential development across the channel from the port. This time business and labor

An aerial view of the north-south main arteries of El Dorado and Center streets in the 1960s shows the park bounded by city hall, the public library, the Civic Auditorium, and a used car lot. Until 1947 McLeod Lake extended through the park area to El Dorado Street. In the background one can see the Stockton Channel and what is left of McLeod Lake. Courtesy, Pacific Center for Western Historical Studies, University of the Pacific

presented a united front before the city council in support of the industrial development and the project was approved. During 1982-1983 modular units were constructed on the site and transferred to barges for shipment to San Francisco Bay and Alaska.

The city promoted innovative solutions to urbanization problems during the 1970s. Both manpower and affirmative action programs were utilized to solve urban ailments. New sewer and water facilities, as well as new streets, met the city's physical needs. A waterfront sea wall and 15 new parks met aesthetic needs. The city continued to annex the bedroom communities to the north. Under the leadership of City Manager Elder Gunter, Stockton applied for and received a large share of federal funds. It was the first city in the nation to receive a Housing and Community Development Block grant. This amounted to $1,803,000, but was only a small

portion of the $82,000,000 in grant funds received during Gunter's seven years as city manager.

There has been a continuing attempt to revitalize downtown, both by the city and federal government. The federal government offered tax incentives to rehabilitate old buildings although, outside of a few newcomers in the community, residents did not launch into these projects until inflation changed the economics of remodeling. It suddenly became more cost-effective to rehabilitate an old downtown building than to build a new one in the north end of town. As refurbished offices became available the legal community moved back into the court-house area.

Grupe Development Company bought and completely remodeled the old high-rise bank building on the corner of Main and Sutter streets. The company used the building for a time, then sold to the State Savings and Loan Association. Soon the rapidly expanding financial institution was renting or buying and refurbishing old buildings all over the area. When the association merged with American Savings and Loan in 1983, downtown Stockton became the headquarters of the largest savings and loan in the nation.

Downtown Stockton had always been a government center, but it gradually became a financial center as well. Office workers flooded the inner city during the day but deserted it at 5 o'clock, returning home to residential areas outside the city. In 1981 an R/UDAT (Regional/Urban Design Assistance Team) study sponsored by the American Institute of Architects was conducted in Stockton. A team of experts swarmed over the inner city for a weekend and came up with an ambitious plan to revitalize the downtown area. The City Planning Commission began designing a completely new city plan along the lines suggested. The plan took two years to formulate and was released in 1983. In the meantime more buildings were being restored to their former beauty and were made functional for modern offices. Hope rose anew for the downtown area.

Politically the city still has its problems, just as it did in the past. Almost every city council in Stockton's history has been fair game for criticism. After all these years the council members are paid only $15 a meeting, but there has been a continuing movement by the business community to increase the pay. Would paying the city council members more money ensure better government? When Elder Gunter, former city manager, was asked that question, he addressed the real problem. "I have always supported better compensation for council members," said Gunter, "but I don't think pay by itself would solve the problem." "What we need is strong community support to back candidates. That would mean district voters should back candidates who look at the overall city as well as their districts." Gunter's answer puts the issue of good government right back where it belongs, in the voters' lap. Only time will tell if the city meets the challenge.

The city's fire department has moved eons from the days of the bucket brigades that dipped water from the Stockton channel. The department has had a class one insurance rating for years; at one time it was only one of five cities in the nation with that honor. A paramedic program has been added in recent years to supplement the city's excellent medical facilities. St. Joseph Hospital's emergency cardiac care and Dameron Hospital's burn unit are among the best. The city's police department has come a long way too, since the corruption of the 1940s.

The cultural life of Stockton is rich. There are 110 churches, which have always had a strong influence in the community, many of them helping to maintain the ethnic heritage of their parishioners. Fine music, dance, and live theater are continuing community programs. The city enjoys an excellent museum and art gallery, Pioneer Museum and Haggin Art Galleries, in Victory Park, and numerous private

Stocktonians saw the Rosenbaum & Crawford Building, built in 1880, razed in 1916. In its place they watched the construction of a granite and brick skyscraper known then as the Farmers & Merchants Bank. Little did architect George W. Kelham know that the building, now the California Building, would be listed on the National Register of Historic Places and is also Stockton Historic Landmark Number 25. Courtesy, Sylvia Sun Minnick

galleries throughout the city add to the cultural diversity. The Stockton City Arts Commission sponsors and encourages artistic endeavors, while the Stockton City Cultural Heritage Board deals with Stockton heritage and historic preservation under the City Planning Commission. This board has been responsible for saving many old Stockton buildings. The group also organized and created the Magnolia Historic District, an area of fine older homes west of California Street and south of Harding Way.

Numerous social and service clubs and lodges have been an integral part of the community throughout its history. Urbanization has not diminished sports participation. Youth groups and sports activities abound. In addition, there are 47 parks, 22 play-grounds, 16 theaters, 5 golf courses, an ice arena and skating rinks, 68 tennis courts, 3 stadiums, 2 large auditoriums, a sports center, and 29 softball diamonds.

During the early 1980s the Stockton Channel was once again crowded with vessels, this time it was pleasure craft lining the shores. Marinas clustered around the city providing hundreds of boat berths. A developer had converted the old grain warehouse into a shopping mall with five restaurants. He built condominium office towers, senior housing and

Above: Within the Catholic cemetery on Harding Way, almost hidden from view by four overgrown juniper trees, the tomb of Charles M. Weber and his family stands as a strong but quiet reminder of the pioneering families who saw the fruition of their dreams in the growth and development of the city of Stockton. Courtesy, Sylvia Sun Minnick

Below: The enlarged Hogan Dam helped but did not halt floods, as this picture of a 1983 flood at Yosemite Lake attests. During that flood high tide reached 10 feet above sea level, reminding Stocktonians that nature's forces are greater than man's means to change the environment. Courtesy, Richard S. Minnick

As the west end of Stockton progressed through redevelopment and old buildings were knocked down by the wrecker's ball, new buildings were erected in their stead. At the head of the channel the multi-roofed Hotel Stockton continues to dominate the skyline unique to Stockton. Courtesy, City Council Chambers

apartments. Optimism prevailed as the Chamber of Commerce moved into the historic warehouse and sponsored a boat show at the yacht harbor. Others built restaurants on the waterfront. One had a great view of McLeod Lake and the other a view west down the channel.

Unfortunately, this major developer who had been the hope of Waterfront revitalization was convicted of sex crimes, served time, was paroled, broke parole and fled the country. He had put all of his assets up for bail, so all of the waterfront property in his name was turned over to the county government. This stalled further development as the property was tied up in red tape for years. The docks deteriorated and no new structures were erected.

Charges of corruption were leveled against four City Council members. One was accused of bribery, fraud and intimidation of voters in a recall election he instituted against another council member. Another faced a misdemeanor conflict of interest charge and was plagued with questions about an obscure charity he controlled. The third was defeated in his fourth term re-election bid because he faced charges of accepting a bribe and was, in fact, convicted of bribery a year later. The fourth was a former mayor who was removed from his council seat by a six to zero vote of the full council. This followed his acquittal on criminal charges that he falsified travel expense documents. He conceded he had altered the document but maintained it was necessary for his investigation into corruption of the

city government. He left the county but was later arrested for drug possession in another county. The city's morale was at an all time low. If a public speaker wanted to get a laugh all one had to do was say "City Council." The public was disgusted.

A City Charter change in 1968 required a member of the Council to be elected by only the voters in the district which he or she represented. So in the 1970s and early '80s most council member looked out for their own districts alone and did not seem to care about what was good for the whole city.

In 1985 a movement arose to change the City Charter once again. A proposed measure called for a change of districts from nine down to six and a mayor elected at large. Voters in each district would vote for candidates in their district at a primary election. The two top candidates in each district would be put to a citywide vote, which would also include the election of the mayor. The following year this measure was put on the ballot for the General Election held on the first Tuesday in November.

VIII.

SOLVING PROBLEMS

November 6, 1986 was another turning point in Stockton's history. Measure C passed by 13.2% margin. Immediately the accusations began to fly. Opponents believed the power of minority citizens to representation on the City Council was diminished. The district boundaries had to be redrawn, because the amendment also changed the number of council members from nine to six plus a mayor.

The boundaries were drawn and approved. Immediately six people, including a City Council member, filed suit against the city, claiming the change to the city charter violated the 1965 Civil Rights Voting Act. The group hired an out-of-state, civil rights attorney. The "Legal Beagle," as he was labeled by the local newspaper, had never lost a civil rights case. Now the City Council was put in the position of being the defendant in the lawsuit. Although the opposing city council member announced no money would go to defend the action, the mayor promised to uphold the new law and defend any action against it.

The opposition used stall tactics to delay the process. A federal judge put a moratorium on any election, until the suit was settled. City Council members remained in office without facing reelection for almost four years. The judge finally upheld Measure C, ruling the plaintiffs had not proved their case and informed the city attorney that no defense was necessary. He reasoned that two of the new city districts were still under minority voter control. He also ordered an election "as soon as practical." An appeal was filed to again delay the process. The appeal was eventually rejected and the election process restarted. Thirty six candidates filed for the districts and mayor of the city. It was in November of 1989 when the election was finally held. The top two candidates in each district and the mayoral race were put on the ballot for the final election held the following February. The new council included both women and ethnic minorities. True to form, Stockton had once again survived a major political crisis.

The worst tragedy in the history of the city occurred on Tuesday, January 17, 1989. A lone gunman opened fire on a playground during an 11:45 a.m. recess at Cleveland Elementary School. Using an AK-47 automatic rifle, he stood for three to four minutes covering the school yard with bullets. He then held the gun to his head, fired and died instantly. Five children were killed, thirty more and a teacher were wounded.

The local Emergency Medical System went into action immediately. Over one hundred paramedics, firemen and police rushed to the scene. Within thirty minutes the teacher and every injured student were on their way to area hospitals located from Modesto on the south to Lodi on the north.

Individuals and groups from inside and outside the community responded with money and aid. Area residents rushed to the local blood bank to donate blood. Counselors and interpreters arrived at the school to help out. The school had a large Asian population which accounted for the fact that all those who died had Asian parents. Six through ten year old students of other nationalities were among the injured. Nine of the injured were released from the hospital immediately. Twenty more and the teacher remained hospitalized.

A view looking west from atop the twelve story, Sutter Office Building. The cleared area in the center of the picture, near the water, is Weber's Point. Construction was in progress to convert the historical site into a park and event center.

The school opened the following day with a bank of counselors on hand to administer personal and classroom therapy. Money poured in and went into a fund to assist those in need.

The community mourned as flags flew at half mast. The Edmonton, Canada Police Department sent a shipment of Teddy Bears, one for each child. A member of the department sent the following message:

"This is an international tragedy. It's terrifying to know it could happen anywhere. We wanted to let those kids know that one bad person doesn't make the whole world bad."

The police investigated, but found no reason for the shootings. The killer left no indication of why he committed this heinous crime. His only connection to the school was that he was enrolled there as a very young child. Toy soldiers and military type camouflage material were found in his room but no note. He had been a troubled youth and had purchased the lethal weapon in Oregon, where he had attended high school. Police investigator learned he was from a broken home with a father who had a history of mental illness.

Some South East Asians outside of Stockton claimed it was a crime of hate, however, evidence was not unearthed to substantiate the charge. A strong anti-automatic weapon movement prevailed in the city. As a result, the Stockton City Council became one of the first in the nation to pass an ordinance banning the sale or possession of automatic weapons. Local officials later appeared before both state and national congressional committees in support of gun control. Following the event, when such shooting happened elsewhere, Stockton officials often received requests for information on how the episode and recovery were handled.

A summer camp group visits the Children's Museum in Stockton. It is a hands-on museum where children can play on a variety of vehicles, do arts and craft and even run a fast food restaurant. The supermarket is a fun attraction where a child can be a customer or a cashier. The museum is run by a non-profit organization and is dedicated to the children who were injured or killed in the school yard shooting in 1989.

A Stockton man, Kenneth Ladd wanted to build a memorial to his deceased wife Nancy Holt Ladd. He made arrangements to donate a large sum of money to the Salvation Army on the condition they build Senior housing in downtown Stockton.

Along with the addition of funds from HUD the organization built this 82 unit apartment building on American Street between Weber Avenue and Channel Street. To qualify, residents need to be low income and a senior 65 or older.

Kaiser Permanente built this new facility to serve patients in this area of Northern California. The building accommodates ninety doctors and full laboratory and radiation services. Note the architectural resemblance to the early day Masonic Temple.

A lasting result from this infamous occurrence was the establishment of a living memorial to the children who died or were injured that day. Led by the wounded teacher, Janet Geng, a Children's Museum was founded in Stockton. The facility was located in a concrete building owned by the city. The structure was in good shape but had been scheduled for demolition in an area development. Today children of all ages learn and play in a delightful atmosphere and attendance continues to grow.

The outpouring of local support and caring is not an unusual occurrence in Stockton. The community has always supported those in need, starting during the Gold Rush when funds were collected to send relief to '49ers struggling over the mountains to California. Fire and other disaster victims have always benefited from the generosity of the community.

In recent times the Stockton community arose to meet the need of a local woman badly burned and stranded in South East Asia. Spearheaded by a local reporter, individuals gave time and money to the cause. A local philanthropist donated the use of his private jet to bring the woman home. Stockton is a community with a heart, there is no doubt.

A no-growth measure had been passed by the 1979 City Council which stymied the addition of new land to the city's general plan. On this issue there was another major voter rebellion at that famous election day in 1986. Voters approved the addition of thousands of acres around the city for future development. Plans moved forward and in 1988 there were 3,998 building permits issued. This figure was up over 1,400 from the previous year. There have been many new developments during the intervening years. A few include; Weston Ranch, Spanos Park, Brookside, La Marada, Harbor Cove, Weber Ranch, Sperry Ranch, Twin Creek Estates, Oak Grove Estates, Bayberry, Ferndale Meadows, Woodsides and Blossom. A huge new retirement complex and senior housing were also built in 1988. In 1991 housing funds were used in South Stockton to in-fill and develop new homes in old neighborhoods.

Home construction was not the only building that was occurring. In 1988 a major new commercial area was opened as the Stockton Auto Center on Hammer Lane, east of West Lane. This was only the beginning, as big box stores were built along the strip. As the Auto Center continued to grow so did the number of warehouse type stores. In-fill along West Lane added more commercial businesses. The city was stretching toward 8 Mile road. To the south at Weston Ranch in 1998 a new commercial district was started with the recent opening of a major grocery store. Gottschalk Department Store came to Stockton in 1988 and was added to the Sherwood Mall. When Macy's and Weinstock's Department stores merged, the local Weinstock's was closed. It was finally replaced by the first Dillard Department Store in California and was attached to the Weberstown Mall.

Growing pains ricochet into all facets of a city. Kaiser Permanente built a new medical facility to accommodate 90 doctors for their area clientele.

St Joseph's Hospital added a new Cancer and Out-Patient Surgery Center and Dameron Hospital also did a major expansion. San Joaquin General Hospital just outside the southern city limits also built a modern facility.

Industrial development kept up the pace too. A unique construction feature, concrete over a plastic bubble, was used for the first time in California at the Port of Stockton. Two of these domes contain live, cold storage facilities. This means that fruit can be moved in and out of storage by remote control, whereas under standard cold storage all the fruit must be removed once the storage unit is opened. A co-generation plant fueled by coal was also constructed at the Port.

The Port Authority will soon be adding Rough and Ready Island, an old naval facility, to its sphere of influence. Part of the Port and other areas of the city are included in an Enterprise Zone established by the State of California. This offers tax credits and financial assistance for employers in new businesses coming into the area.

Stockton has been a transportation hub since the Gold Rush. Over the years traffic problems had increased, so in 1990 voters passed a half cent sales tax to meet these needs. A major obstacle was alleviated

with completion of the Crosstown Freeway in 1993. It is the shortest link north of Los Angeles of super-highways 99 and Interstate 5. The concept linking the two highways was adopted in 1953. There were no agreements made until 1963. Construction was started and halted when Federal Funds were frozen in the early 1970s. Governor Jerry Brown's administration vowed no more money for completed or incompleted freeways. The Crosstown Freeway was completed from Fresno Avenue to Stanislaus Street where it hung in space. A community activist and local radio station owner, Ort Loftus, led F. O. C. U. S. (Finish Our Crosstown, Unite Stockton) a committee to see the project resumed. The group collected 27,000 signatures on petitions to complete what Loftus called the "Freeway to Nowhere." Hope was revived in 1983 when George Deukmejian was running for the office of Governor. He promised completion of the link, if elected. Three months after the election he ordered California Transportation Department to resume construction. The project was originally estimated to be completed in 1970 at a cost of $50,000,000. When it was finally finished in 1993 the bill came to $140,000,000. A grand celebration was held and the new highway was named "The Ort Loftus Freeway." The new link changed the travel time across some parts of the city from twenty five minutes to less than five minutes.

As more and more people moved into Stockton, the stress on education facilities also became greater. This was spread out over the four school districts in the city. Stockton Unified School District dropped cross-town busing to return to neighborhood schools. The district has one new Elementary School under construction to open in 1999 and one on the planning boards. Lincoln Unified built a new elementary school in the Brookside area. Manteca Unified School District built one elementary school in the Weston Ranch area and another will open in 1999. Lodi Unified impacted by the growth in extreme north Stockton area, built the new Bear Creek High School. They have also added one middle school and seven elementary schools. The school's have carried the burden but they have also benefited from a new bedroom tax added to building fees for new homes.

The new Bear Creek High School in North Stockton. It is the Lodi Unified School District which also constructed a new Middle School and seven Elementary schools in the area in the last ten years. The school team are called the Bruins.

Delta Community College met the needs of the city and area students, not only as preparation for Universities but also offered job-training courses. Many two year courses prepared students for jobs in a wide range of occupations. A fast version of these programs was put into effect in 1998 when CALWORKS (California Work Opportunity and Responsibility to Kids) a welfare-reform program was initiated. All the new classes are designed to get welfare recipients into the work force as soon as possible. Study areas include nine-week courses in: basic culinary arts, nursing, early-childhood education, office and retail trades, key data entry, bookkeeping and private security. A normal two year landscaping course was reduced to no more than a year.

A major new thrust in public education for the city, occurred when the State of California decided to vacate the old State Hospital Grounds. Captain Charles M. Weber had deeded half of the present site to the State originally, so it had to be kept in public domain. The State turned the land and buildings over to the California State University System. Stanislaus State College had been holding classes at Delta College and switched to the new site. S.S.C. opened the new satellite campus in the fall of 1998 with 1,000 students in upper division graduate and credential programs. Designated as the lead campus, S.S.C. operates the full 103 acre facility.

Following the bloom of the gold era, agriculture had

Crowds fill the Asparagus Festival grounds at Oak Grove Regional Park. Asparagus Alley is in the foreground. A record high of 80,000 people attended in 1998. It took 4,700 volunteers donating 25,000 hours to staff the event. Courtesy, Asparagus Festival Committee.

come into its own as the major producer of income for Stockton during the remainder of of the 19th Century. Naturally, the machine shops in the city were major players in the mechanization of agriculture. Agriculture remained supreme in importance until World War II. During this war the city's interest shifted to military installations and war production. Following the war, with many new residents, the local focus was directed to other areas. The destruction of Stockton's infamous "Skid Row" in the '50s and '60s, was followed by a strong urbanization movement in the 1970s. Much of the populous began to believe the city was no longer dependent on agriculture.

In the mid 1980s various factors, including high interest rates, hurt the agriculture community. Many farmers went out of business or sought extra jobs. By the end of the 1980s the industry began to recover. Production values rose until 1995 when agriculture production in the county topped one billion dollars in annual income. All of this in spite of the fact that farm land was disappearing under new housing on a regular basis. The agriculture income figure continued

Farmers at the annual Stockton Ag Expo look over every conceivable product, service or supply for their needs. The show covers over 250,000 square feet at the San Joaquin County Fairgrounds. It is sponsored by, and photo courtesy of, the Greater Stockton Chamber of Commerce.

to rise. The last reporting year was 1997, when farming in San Joaquin County earned $1,400,000,000 (1.4 billion). This is gross income from raw agriculture products, and does not include food processing or other related industries. Economists use a multiplier number of four to this amount to get the eventual economic impact on the area.

The Greater Stockton Chamber of Commerce has sponsored "Stockton Ag Expo," a farm show, in the city for twenty two years. Farmers attend to see machinery, services and supplies from local, state and international companies. It is a regional show which draws farmers from a wide area, even though its primary target is within one hundred miles of the city. This region produced over $11,000,000,000 (eleven billion) in agricultural income in 1997. Civic leaders are once again recognizing the importance of agriculture to Stockton's "well being."

One locally grown agriculture product has become the feature of a major annual celebration. Originally under the sponsorship of the Visitors Bureau, the first Asparagus Festival was held in 1986. Now a single non-profit organization runs the event, however, one hundred local non-profit organizations share in the income. In 1987 it was rated among the top festivals

in the nation by a trade magazine, *Events Business News.* At the 1998 event 4,700 volunteers worked 25,000 hours serving the 80,000 people in attendance. The festival also has contributed to improving Stockton's image.

The Greater Stockton Chamber of Commerce also staged the "Stockton Sport and Boat Show" on the waterfront for nine years. A showcase of day cruisers and luxury yachts, it drew visitors from a wide area. Its demise came when the federal government imposed a ten percent luxury tax on any purchase of $100,000 or more. The boat business languished and many dealers went out of business.

Other trade shows are held regularly at the San Joaquin County Fairgrounds facilities. San Joaquin County Fair still has live horse races during the annual event, but they also have an off-track betting facility utilized year round. The Fair was held in August for many years but was moved to a June date. Attendance continues to rise with headline entertainment as a major attraction.

According to the National Weather Service, Stockton's annual average rain fall is 13.88 inches, calculated from July 1 through June 30. In 1986 a major flood occurred in the north end of the county. During February, storm after storm rolled into the area from the Pacific Ocean. Thornton at the northern edge

Panella Company trucks are ready to leave for the tomato fields of Northern California. Ralph Panella who founded this company initiated the use of these large bins. The company operates trucks, with 400 dual bin trailers. With two major highway systems running through the city, Stockton is a major center for the trucking industry, including both long and short haul carriers. There are over two hundred trucking companies in the Metropolitan area alone.

of San Joaquin County flooded and major highways were closed down for five days. The California Department of Water Resources targeted the Mokelumne River for long range flood protection. In spite of this very wet year, another drought occurred over the next three years when the annual rainfall dropped to 64% of normal.

The next major flood occurred south of Stockton in January 1997. The flood was the result of a warm rain falling at the 7,000 foot level in the mountains. It melted a heavy snow pack causing the Sacramento and San Joaquin Rivers to overflow. In spite of the flooding the annual rainfall for 1996-1997 was a meager 9.82 inches. In 1997-1998, El Nino delivered a near record total of 18.40 inches at the airport weather station, but even more at the Fire Station near Delta College. That particular annual reading was a whopping 32.61 inches. These two weather reporting stations are approximately ten miles apart. In the past, individuals noted that the airport weather report

Stockton's newest fire station. Station #14 is located just north of the new Bear Creek High School and a half mile from the city's northern boundary on 8 Mile Road. Firemen interrupted their lunch hour to pull the truck out for this picture.

California Ammonia's unique storage domes are located at the Port of Stockton. The construction of concrete over an originally inflated plastic bubble contains unincumbered space inside. Association growers' fruits and vegetables are moved into and out of storage by remote control.

was always low compared to other local rain gauges in north Stockton. A retired meteorologist who worked at the airport station was asked why this happened. He said he believed that the airport was in the rain shadow of Mt. Diablo, meaning the mountain took the rain out of the clouds before they got to the airport.

Fortunately in spite of this heavy rainfall, no flooding occurred in the spring of 1998. The heavy rains and late spring weather did manage to hurt farming once again by eliminating and/or delaying crops.

Water continues to be major factor in the city's health. The only city in California's Great Valley without a source of snow water runoff, the city still depends on groundwater. Stockton East Water District continues to work toward a more lasting water supply, but has had little success. The district made an agreement with the Federal Bureau of Reclamation to receive water from the new Molones Dam on the Stanislaus River. The government agency told local officials to prepare to receive water. The district dug a tunnel to carry the water to Woodward Dam in the east side of the county. While they were doing this, the Federal policy was changed to take water out of the same watershed to protect fish in the river and the tunnel remained dry. Winter water could be released into the tunnel but there is no storage to hold it, so the problems continue.

The Stockton Fire Department was compelled to grow with the city's expansion. Two new stations were established. One was placed adjacent to Bear Creek High School and another in Weston Ranch. Rough and Ready Island was added and a Water Rescue unit of

Customers enjoy a lake-side luncheon in north Stockton. Ducks that live on Quail Lake regularly mooch snacks from customers.

divers became available for underwater search in the Delta and nearby lakes. To meet modern needs, a Hazardous Waste unit was also established. Both fire fighters and trucks have increased in numbers. In 1984 two women were hired for the first time one of them reached the rank of Captain in 1998. Since 1984 black men have been hired and also have achieved officer status. Unfortunately two firemen were killed in a house fire in 1997.

The Stockton Police Department is a long ways from the Alcalde law of 1848. The department now has 372 officers and enough waiting for approval to make a total of 394. there has also been many changes under Police Chief Ed Chavez. Department employees are a greater ethnic mixture than in the past. In December 1997 there were 56% black males and 13% black females as dispatchers or patrol officers. Hispanics represented the second largest group with males accounting for 11.8% and females 3.3% females. Whites, both male and female, only account for 7.1% and another 7.1% represent other ethnic groups.

Serious crimes have gone down from 97 murders

committed in 1984 to a low of 44 in 1996. Gang activity has been cut back by special task forces to deal with the problem. The Police Department has many more public service programs than in the past. These include: Chaplin Service, Citizen Ride-Along, Citizen Academy, Copp's Training, Senior Awareness Program, Safe Neighborhood, Neighborhood Watch and others. In its effort to surpress gangs the department has become much more involved with youth programs. These include Safe Kids Academy, Rotary Read In, Bike Rodeo, Junior Cadet and Red Ribbon Drug Free Programs to name a few.

During the 1980s the city had received a tremendous amount of bad publicity, which in turn generated a poor self-image among local residents. In 1986 an

The city slogan is displayed on a Stockton Water Tank just west of Interstate 5. The slogan was selected in a contest staged by the local Convention and Visitors Bureau. It calls attention to the fact that ocean going vessels sail into Stockton through a deep-water channel of the San Joaquin River.

ad-hock committee was organized to launch a positive publicity campaign. Entitled "Stockton's Great. Take a Look," it involved all sorts of publicity in newspaper, magazines, radio and television. The Convention Bureau ran a competition to come up with a new slogan for the city. The winner suggested "Stockton, California's Sunrise Seaport." The first edition of this book was used as an argument before the city council when they voted and accepted the motto. This slogan plays on the fact that most people outside of the city do not realize that ocean ships sail this far inland.

Sports have long been important in this town where a single game inspired the noted poem Casey at the Bat by a San Francisco sports writer, Ernest Thayer. The Stockton Ports baseball team is a AAA franchise team of the Milwaukee Brewers National League team. The latest owners are the younger generation of the famous O'Malley baseball family, former owners of the Los Angeles Dodgers. A current campaign is underway to build a new baseball stadium near the Stockton waterfront.

Team sports draw thousands of players annually from sub-teens to senior citizens. Many individuals have gone on to excel on a national level. Currently, three

Above: Friends stop for a visit at the Maxwell's Book Store and Sidewalk Cafe on the Miracle Mile. This was Stockton's first shopping district outside of downtown and is located on Pacific Avenue, once known as the Lincoln

Highway (Hwy. 50) The shopping area was in decline, so the area merchants banded together to revitalize it. They sponsor a sidewalk sale every Thursday evening during the summer months.

Below: Jerry Rice, San Francisco 49er wide receiver goes out for a pass during practice at the University of the Pacific in July 1998. The former Super Bowl Champion team's man- agement signed a ten year

agreement to hold their annual summer training camp at the University of the Pacific starting in 1998. Photograph courtesy of Stockton, San Joaquin Convention & Visitors Bureau.

The new eight story Washington Mutual Building viewed from the top of the parking garage on Market street in Stockton. The building was started by American Saving and Loan that failed, but fortunately the $40,000,000 building was completed by the new owner. It covers a full block of downtown Stockton.

pro baseball players, one pro football player, and the nation's top Pro-bowler call Stockton their home town.

The University of the Pacific administration dropped its football team, but both the men's basketball team and the women's volleyball teams have flourished. In the 1998 during the National Pro Basketball Draft, one of U. O. P's team members was the number one pick. The University also became the center of attention in the fall of 1997 when the San Francisco 49er Football team announced they were looking for a new training camp. After much jockeying for position by various cities, Stockton won. A major factor in the city's selection was the assistance received from a local resident, and owner of the San Diego Chargers, Alex

Spanos. Even though his team is a rival of the San Francisco team, he used his personal influence with the 49er's management. He also contributed one million dollars to the University coffers to help upgrade campus facilities for the camp. The team arrived in Stockton on July 17, 1998.

American Savings and Loan became a key player in decaying downtown Stockton in the 1980s. The company had originally started in Stockton as State Savings and Loan. Through acquisitions and and mergers the company became American Savings. It was eventually the largest Saving and Loan in the country to be bailed out by federal funds. In 1996 the company became part of Washington Saving Bank. In the 1980s Stockton was deteriorating. American Savings and Loan was growing and moved into most of the empty office buildings in the downtown area. The company also purchased the old bank building on the corner of Sutter and Main Street. Plans were made for a modern building on the diagonal block. Fortunately when the company failed, the work continued under new ownership. The $40 million structure was completed and the city built a new parking structure

Stockton Police Department patrolmen cruse downtown. Here they are checking our the parking lot at the Waterfront Warehouse on West Weber Avenue. Downtown merchants agree they have been a good influence in the area.

across the street. This was the first new structure in downtown Stockton since the redevelopment of old Skid Row. Some feared that the Stockton newspaper, *The Record*, would leave downtown, however the Omaha company owners have purchased expansion property nearby.

San Joaquin County government also contributed to the revitalization of downtown with the construction of a new Human Resources Building and another new parking structure. They also vacated the old Hotel Stockton, which is still empty but available for development. In 1998 city development money was available to business owners to upgrade long neglected buildings. This coupled with a crack down on code violation by the city staff made a difference. Bicycle patrolmen were put in the city core. New property owners moved into downtown, as real estate bargains were picked up by out-of-town buyers.

Weber's Point, the site of Captain Weber's original home, had become an eyesore after the Holiday Inn closed and was demolished. It become a weed infested garbage dump. The mayor organized a Waterfront Development Task Force. One of the first acts was a clean-up day, with volunteers doing the job. The

Lake-shore living is a way of life for many Stockton Residents. There are seven lakes in Stockton surrounded by single family homes, condominiums and apartments and even some businesses.

committee met on a regular basis, working with a consulting firm and citizen input. A master plan was developed with the recommendation that entertainment centers, ball park, museums etc. be located on the south side of the channel and condominiums on the north side. The point itself is being converted into a park and event center.

The committee also recommended uncovering Stockton Slough between El Dorado and Center Streets and installing a decorative fountain. One major problem facing the committee was cleaning up the water in McLeod Lake and the head of Stockton Channel. The problem is being approached but not solved to date. The city issued orders to repair the dock at the Waterfront Yacht Harbor or take them out of the water. Needless to say the docks were restored. As this book goes to press the task force continues to meet on a regular basis with the city staff.

The World Wildlife Museum also draws visitors to the Waterfront. The Museum began with a single

This Golden Takin is the only mounted specimen of the animal outside of China. On display at the World Wildlife Museum in Stockton, it is a rare species of the goat family, only recently discovered in the White Mountains of Western China. Courtsey, Robert Beckrest, Beckrest Advertising & Design.

A herd of Greater Kudu on display in the World Wildlife Museum located in Stockton. The museum is affiliated with the Smithsonian Institute. Courtesy of Robert Beckrest, Beckrest Advertising & Design.

collection by Jack Perry, a local resident. The collection continued to grow until today there are more than 5,000 mounted animals in the collection. Still in temporary housing, the museum has 2,000 mounted animals on display. Many rare animals are on display including the only Golden Takin in existence outside of its native country, China. An African elephant, measuring twelve feet high at the shoulders is the latest acquisition.

In the summer of 1998 it was announced that the World Wildlife Museum in Stockton had become associated with the Smithsonian Institute. Future plans have the museum animals and staff playing an active role in traveling displays and educational program planned for students in 240,000 schools. In the beginning there are to be three such project in California and one of them will be in Stockton.

Perhaps one move that did more than any other to get people downtown, was the leasing of the Fox California Theater by the city. A promotional director was hired to book appearances. Crews from the California Conservation Corps vacuumed seats and carpets, they removed gum, scrubbed floors, and painted. No structural changes were made, but the grand old theater came back into its own. The

promoter booked Las Vegas style headline acts. There was a grand celebration on opening night with the San Francisco company of "Beach Blanket Babylon." The Convention and Visitors Bureau sponsored an "Art Deco Ball" in Hunters square. Dinner was served before the show and followed by dancing in the square. Just like the original opening of the theater in 1930, some people could not get inside and were entertained in the square. Since that auspicious occasion, headline acts have filled the theater time and time again. Big bands and rock groups appeared on stage, as did comedians, famous singers and musicians. Some headline acts included: Natalie Cole, Johnny Mathis, Tom Jones, Dave Brubeck, Victor Borge, Ray Charles and many more.

The Downtown Stockton Alliance, a new non-profit organization was formed to promote, develop and maintain Stockton's central area. Its goal is to expand an aggressive marketing program to attract new business into the 60 block core of the city. Maintenance crews work on a daily litter abatement, steam cleaning and pressure washing sidewalks. The area took on a brighter look because of private business restoration projects. Hospitality guides walk a twenty-four block area, greeting visitors and lending assistance where necessary. Certified Farmers' Markets are held under the freeway and in Hunter Square on a regular

Below: The snack shack at Billy Hebert Field, home of the Stockton Ports AAA baseball club which operates under the Milwaukee Brewers farm system. The name Mudville comes from the famous poem "Casey At The Bat," written about a baseball game once played in Stockton.

Above: A melon grower helps a customer at the Friday noon Farmers Market held on Main Street in downtown Stockton. The weekly market is sponsored by the Stockton Downtown Alliance.

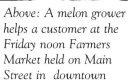

basis. Special events have included a street fair and automobile show. Guided tours are conducted once a month. A local historical society held a fund raising dinner in a tent in the middle of Main Street.

The greatest deterrent to the downtown area is the stubborn attitude of many north Stockton residents who believe the area is dangerous. Unfortunately, children have been raised in the area, with the admonition, "Don't go south of Harding Way." Yet others have learned it is a safe environment which gets better all of the time, according to downtown workers.

As downtown strives to rebound, the rest of the city flourishes. The Stockton Symphony plays to sell-out crowds both in regularly scheduled concerts at Atherton Theater and special events such as the

Pixi Woods, a children park and playground is always a cool place for summer fun. The park contains a variety of playground equipment and features a train and riverboat ride. It also has a special Birthday

Party House where many local children celebrate their big days. It is run by a non-profit organization for the enjoyment of the children in the area. Pictured here are three children climbing aboard a stagecoach.

concerts in the park. The 9th Annual Pops & Picnic concert staged in the Civic Auditorium in 1998 was once again a sell-out event. The Stockton Chorale a group of one hundred and twenty five singers not only give local concerts but also in other parts of the world. In 1998 they performed in both England and Wales. San Joaquin Delta College Art Department stages six to ten stage productions annually. Stockton Civic Theater runs both winter and summer with local talent. The Stockton Ballet is alive and well and includes national and international dancers in their annual Christmas production.

A few years ago a Stanford University research group released a report that Stockton's ethnic mixture was exactly what the national mixture will be in the future. The research was flawed. By using the city figures the researchers disregarded the fifty to sixty thousand people who live in the metropolitan areas adjacent to the city.

By 1989 the population figures for the Stockton City limits was 192,300. The Metropolitan area including the city and suburbs from 8 Mile Road on the north, to the French Camp road on the south, was estimated at over 240,000. The 1998 figures from a Stockton Planning Department spokesman shows a dramatic increase. The new estimated figures have the city population alone at 240,000 and the metropolitan area as approximately 300,000 people.

Today Stockton Channel is once again crowded with vessels, this time with pleasure craft lining the shore. Marinas cluster around the city providing hundreds of boat berths. Boats can cruise into McLeod Lake to the site where trappers once met.

The old grain warehouse on the waterfront has been converted into business offices, a shop, two restaurants, a hot dog stand and the home of the Greater Stockton Chamber of Commerce. The West-End Redevelopment project now includes luxury condominium office towers, senior citizen housing, apartment complexes and the Children's and Wildlife Museums. Stockton is changing and growing as it becomes increasingly urbanized.

What does the future hold for the city? There is no doubt it will continue to grow. Current population trends show California's Central Valley will continue to grow and Stockton is a part of that growth pattern. The city has always been flexible, yielding to the tide of events and answering the needs around it. There is no reason to believe this will change.

The words of early settler Charles Grunsky, written in a letter home to Germany on January 19, 1851 proved him to be a prophet:

I may be wrong, but I confess that I have great faith in the future of this beautiful country. I believe that in time it will be the foremost state in the union. With the resources of this state, tremendous progress can be made. There will soon be talk of a railroad from New York to San Francisco, Sacramento or Stockton. A railroad thousand of miles of which will pass through a vast extent of uninhabited wilderness and will cross the Sierra Nevada.

Here was a man of vision who had faith in the city of Stockton, for he selected it as his home. Others followed and made the city what it is today.

The unique combination of land and water in the Stockton area has attracted man from the beginning of the region's history. Today Stockton is a cosmopolitan city which accepts new people, never promising a paradise but offering a refuge, where each must earn his place. It is a vital, thriving place where the land nurtures abundance as each day the sun rises over the majestic Sierra Nevada mountain range, reaches it zenith over the city, and sets behind the Diablo Range into the sunset sea. Stockton, born in the California Gold Rush, is ready for the 21st Century.

This boat owner only needs to go out his back door to board his boat and cruse the 1,000 miles of the San Joaquin/Sacramento Delta. It is also possible to cruise into San Francisco and out the Golden Gate, just 70 nautical miles to the west.

VIII.
CHRONICLES OF LEADERSHIP

During the California Gold Rush days Stockton Channel, stemming some two and one-half miles from the San Joaquin River to mid-Stockton, was the head of navigation for paddle-wheel and side-wheel steamboats and sailing vessels carrying fortune hunters from San Francisco bound for the Mother Lode and High Sierra goldfields. Those gold seekers accounted for Stockton's commercial beginnings by their purchases of picks and shovels, boots and woolens, buggies, wagons and horses, and food—to say nothing of their patronization of local saloons.

Many luckless prospectors returned to chop down thousands of oak trees surrounding Stockton to reap the golden harvests of farming, thus starting the city on its way to becoming the center of one of the richest agricultural areas in the nation: San Joaquin County produced nearly $1.4 billion in crops in 1997.

The area's soil yields scores of crops, led by grapes, milk, nuts, fruit, tomatoes and asparagus. Early-day flour mills have been replaced by feed mills, corn products, walnut-and meat-processing plants, canneries, frozen-food plants and packing houses.

Agriculture led to industry, the first factories manufacturing farm machinery and implements as the pioneers dug for crops rather than gold. Stockton now has approximately 500 industries, including products for aerospace, illuminated glass, cement pipe, steel-fabrication and wood products and wineries to list a few.

Major industries in the area include warehousing and distribution centers. New warehouses have been added every year since the completion of Interstate Highway 5. Both old and new industrial companies are rapidly expanding. During 1997-1998, 12 companies invested $22.7 million in new or improved facilities.

Today Stockton is the head of navigation for seagoing cargo ships that dock at the Port of Stockton, the city's first and foremost inland seaport, created by converting the San Joaquin River into a 35-foot ship channel. Stressing bulk cargo, the port loads and unloads cargoes for ships that sail the seven seas and is served by two transcontinental railroads. Over 250 local, state and national trucking companies operate out of the area.

Financial transactions are conducted by several hundred banks, savings and loan agencies, credit unions, and lending agencies that offer all manner of loans, from personal to homeowner, from crop to business.

The fine local educational system is enhanced by San Joaquin Delta College, a community college, Stanislaus State College and University of the Pacific, the second-oldest institution of higher learning in California. Stockton boasts theater, ballet, symphony, an art league, museums and art galleries for the culturally minded. Sports fans can witness events in all major fields and there are facilities available for tennis, golf, swimming, softball, soccer and bowling, as well as numerous parks for picnicking.

The organizations you will meet on the following pages have chosen to support this important civic event. They are representative of the businesses that have helped to make "Stockton, Someplace Special," with the talent, skills, and determination that are the lifeblood of a thriving community.

Stockton's growth escalated more in the 15 years between 1960 and 1975 than it had in the previous 100 years, and continues to do so. This aerial view of downtown Stockton occurred prior to the West End Redevelopment program the city underwent in the mid-1960s and 1970s. Clearly in view is Washington Square, once the location of the Agricultural Pavilion, and to its left is Chinatown. The Civic Auditorium, Hotel Stockton, the back of the courthouse, and Cunningham's Castle (County Jail) are also in view. Courtesy, Stockton Chamber of Commerce

ACME TRUCK PARTS & EQUIPMENT, INC.

Acme Truck Parts & Equipment is celebrating its 75th year in Stockton. Founded in 1923 by Sol Davidson who became interested in trucks after driving an ambulance in World War I, the business has grown from a small store at 324 S. Center Street to the largest supplier of new, used and rebuilt truck parts in Northern California. In the early years, the shop was open seven days a week, dismantlers were paid $20 per week and a good salesman could earn $30 per week.

Davidson's son, Al, entered the business in 1949 after graduating from UC Berkeley with a degree in mechanical engineering. Soon after the auto parts busineee was sold and the name was changed to Acme Truck Parts & Equipment to better describe the activities of the firm. Property acquired in 1936 at 1016 South Wilson Way (Highway 99 at that time) became the main location. The company still does truck dismantling in the eastern portion of the yard, but now the company also sells new truck parts and specializes in rebuilding of

Nathan Davidson, vice-president.

Andy Grutman, president and CEO.

truck components for medium and heavy duty trucks.

Acme's truck sales fill a special niche for farmers, contractors and any business where trucks and equipment are needed. In June 1998, Acme opened a 3 1/2 acre truck and equipment sales yard adjoining I-5 Freeway, just 1/2 mile south of downtown Stockton. At this location, the sales department is headed by Nathan Davidson, vice president and a third generation to the 75 year old company. Here customers can purchase dump trucks, flat bed trucks, crane trucks, basket trucks, trailers and other specialized vehicles. With Acme's shop facilities, any of these vehicles can be modified to fit the special needs of the customer.

Andy Grutman, 24 years with the company, is now the president and CEO. Under his leadership, the business has continued to grow. The drive train rebuilding shop has

expanded. A power steering gear shop with testing equipment has been installed. A machine shop with an AxiLine propeller shaft rebuilding unit can produce dynamically balanced and tested units. Acme is now an authorized rebuilding and warranty station for Allison automatic transmissons for trucks and off-highway application.

Other affiliates include Acme Lift Trucks, Inc. in Stockton specializing in the sale of forklifts, material handling equipment, and hydraulic components and Specialty Truck Parts, Inc. in San Jose and San Leandro. Al Davidson is chairman of the board of the three corporations.

Acme has built its business of 75 years on a policy of customer satisfaction and good service at a fair price. Its many repeat customers offer proof that Acme is properly meeting the challenge of today's competitive markets and will continue to do so in the 21st century.

Acme Truck Parts & Equipment, Inc. proudly celebrates its 75th anniversary in 1998.

AD ART/ELECTRONIC SIGN CORPORATION

Founded in 1958, Ad Art/Electronic Sign Corporation began as a small electric sign business in neighboring Modesto under the leadership of founder, Lou A. Papais, his brother, John, and close friend, Dan O'Leary. By 1960, the firm had outgrown its original plant and relocated to larger quarters on Miner Street in Stockton. The three owners coupled inventive sign concepts with sophisticated selling techniques and quickly propelled the fledgling California concern into national prominence.

Over the past three decades, Ad Art has consistently led the industry in the introduction of innovative technologies and sign applications. In the late '60s and early '70s, Ad Art was first to

Ad Art's 1995 Weberstown Mall sign, on Pacific Avenue, was the first full-color electronic message display in California. Photo by Charles Barnard

offer West Coast manufacturing programs to major sign users, such as Chevron, Wells Fargo and McDonald's. Their association with the world's largest fast-food chain now spans seventeen years with Ad Art-built signs being installed in 20 countries, including China, Israel and Hong Kong. The Stockton-based firm also was an early developer of electronic message systems and was the first in the industry to install a comprehensive CAD-CAM system for design and manufacturing. In the early '80s Ad Art collaborated with the 3M Company in the exploration of translucent film on plastic, producing prototype signs for Bank of America in the process. This pioneering film technology has now become the manufacturing standard for the industry.

The year 1983 signaled Ad Art's entry into the international sign market when it collaborated with the Bechtel Corporation in the creation of over 20,000 signs at the King Khalid International airport in Riyadh, Saudi Arabia—a two-year, $14 Million project that established Ad Art's credentials as a major world-class sign producer.

Since its incorporation, Ad Art's award-winning designers and craftsmen have repeatedly contributed to the exotic signscape of Las Vegas where the Company has secured an historic presence. Beginning with the Thunderbird, Caesar's Palace, Frontier, Stardust and Flamingo—in the mid '60s—Ad Art racked up one award-winning success after another with a list of spectacular achievements that currently include the Golden Nugget, Excalibur, Mirage, Treasure Island, Monte Carlo, Rio, Las Vegas Convention Center and Bellagio. In the process, Ad Art has designed, engineered, manufactured and installed most of the World's tallest electric signs, including the famed Stardust, the Superdome in New

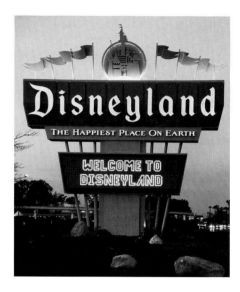

Disneyland's primary marquee spectacular, manufactured and installed by Ad Art in 1989. Photo by W.R. Hannapple

Orleans and M-G-M supersigns. Many of these remarkable icons utilize the firm's fourth-generation electronic message systems, providing TV-like full-color imagery through technologies developed at Ad Art's 120,000 square foot headquarters along Highway 99. Weberstown Mall on Pacific Avenue received the first full-color electronic message display in California and the firm's advanced, full-color L.E.D. system is the first to be installed in the state, at Serramonte Center in Daly City. Its athletic stadium and arena displays are distributed world-wide through associates in Britain, Mexico, Brazil, the Middle East and Russia.

Ad Art celebrates its 40th year in business with over 300 employees, branch offices in Los Angeles, San Francisco, Las Vegas and Fresno, and annual sales nearing $45 Million. As the major participant in a March 1998 merger with publicly-held Display Technologies (DTEK), Ad Art continues to maintain its position as one of the nation's premier sign companies and the largest in the Golden State.

B & B FARMS

After World War II, Arrny Air Corps veteran Albert Brocchini owned the Swiss American Club in Manteca. When his son Robert was born in November 1947, Albert decided to start farming because he didn't want his children to say their dad worked in a bar. His first crop in the summer of 1948 was 20 acres of watermelons.

It was a one-man operation from the hoe to irrigation to harvest. He worked at the bar in the evenings and farmed during the day. In order to irrigate, Albert said he would take off his shoes and socks, and sleep in the field with his feet in the (irrigation) check. When the water reached the end of the row, it would wake him up and he would shovel the dirt to change the flow to the next check.

In 1950 he formed a partnership with his brother and added the Hardware Mart in Manteca to the business. Brocchini Brothers continued to grow a little bit each year as property became available. Albert laughs as he remembers going to the bank for a loan when he decided to expand his operation. It was a big jump from an $8,000 operating loan to a $20,000 request for financing. In those days, all loan requests had to be approved by the main branch in San Francisco, and Albert was turned down for the increase. The bank felt that there really was no future in farming in California, but that

if he wanted to start a new business in town, maybe a used car lot or something else, the bank would reconsider!

Albert found new financing from a different bank, and started expanding. He was always thinking about, or looking for a new crop. Bob says that he couldn't think of a single crop that his dad didn't consider growing. Anything was possible. Always a progressive farmer, Albert started fall bedding for tomatoes, which was questioned at the time, but is now an accepted statewide practice.

Over the years, the farming has included a cattle operation and row crops including those first watermelons, sweet potatoes, yams, cannery and fresh market tomatoes, honeydews, onions, bell peppers, carrots, pimientos, chives, sugar beets and others. Alfalfa, corn, barley, oats and wheat figured into the rotation plan.

Considered an innovator in mechanization, Brocchini Farms owned the first mechanized cucumber harvester in California in the early '60s. His strawberry crops during the '60s traveled far and wide when he started growing for both fresh and frozen markets. One of Bob's high school buddies talks about unloading supplies in Viet Nam, while serving in the Marines, and was surprised to see "Brocchini Bros. Strawberries" on the can of frozen berries. The oldest of five children, son Bob, joined him in the farming operation after graduation from Cal Poly in December 1969.

Albert Brocchini, founder of B & B Farms.

Brocchini Bros. gave way to Albert Brocchini Farms, Inc., better known as B &B Farms. The home-place moved from Manteca to Ripon, and expansion continued with almonds, wine grapes, cherries, walnuts and apples. Growing, packing and marketing their own B & B onions as Mid Cal Produce, and partnership in an apple packing and shipping operation demonstrate a progressive attitude towards growth and variety in their operation.

Community involvement is a family tradition and includes the Strawberry Advisory Commission, California Tomato Research Association, Farm Bureau at the local and state levels, Manteca and Ripon School Boards, and active support for FFA and 4-H, Manteca Chamber of Commerce and other service clubs. Albert and Bob, both inductees in the Agricultural Hall of Fame in San Joaquin County are now joined in the farming operation by the third generation: Michelle, a 1994 Cal Poly ag grad, and Stephen, a 1998 Chico State ag grad.

From a one-man operation in 1948 of 20 rented acres to a family farming corporation which owns 3,500 acres, and hires 50 year-round employees and about 270 employees during the peak harvest season, B & B Farms is proud of a 50 year history of farming in San Joaquin County.

Three generations of Brocchini's: Albert, grandson Steve, son Bob, and grand-daughter Michelle.

I. B. BENEDICT INC.

I. B. Benedict who had once installed headlights and batteries in horseless carriages, opened an automotive shop in 1937. He specialized in parts and repairs of carburetors and electric work. He survived WWII when there was much work but few parts and incorporated in 1948. The company built a reputation for good work and employed ten men by 1960.

In 1961 Tom Wilson went to work as a parts counter person, progressed to outdoor sales and was named manager in 1978. The company was still operating out of the small shop on Miner Avenue in Stockton at that time. Wilson wanted to expand, but was told he would have to buy the company to achieve that goal. He approached fellow employees, Carl Barbieri, Joel Mauser, Ernie Hall and others who agreed to invest. He sold all his property, obtained a bank loan and the group purchased the company with Wilson buying the majority share. The new owners expanded the variety of parts and soon built a 20,000 square foot facility on East Miner Avenue and opened a branch in Modesto.

One of Wilson's first acts was to initiate an employee profit sharing plan. He had two goals: the best employees and a good customer base. Training became company policy. Both owners and employees participate in the training programs, which include business

I.B. Benedict Co. Auto Parts.

I.B. Benedict Co.

practices, computers, electronics, suspension and fuel systems and the newer ABS (Automatic Braking Systems). Every employee learns that the customer is number one. The company invests in its customers too, by offering technical training and incentives.

Today the company that grossed $1,000,000 in 1979 now does $10,000,000 of business a year. They have become the dominant parts house in a market that has seen a major decline of the independents over the last six years. A new branch was opened in Galt this past year. Today the company has 50 employees, many of which have many years with the company. The three partners, Barbieri, Hall and Mauser are all working outside sales which very likely

accounts for the staying power of the company. Wilson is president of the corporation.

The company has joined many automotive industry organizations and Wilson has done more than his share of leadership. He is past president of the California Automotive Wholesale Association and the State of California Automotive Credit Union. He currently serves on the board of governors of the National Association of Automotive Warehouse Distributors. He is a past president of the Kiwanis Club of Stockton and devotes his and the company efforts to many community service projects. Sponsored events include: races at the local speedway, golf tournaments, Air shows, and celebrity appearances. Most of these activities have raised money for local worthy causes, ie: science classes, child abuse prevention programs etc.

Tom Wilson and his wife Pat have two daughters, Trisha Rocha and Windy Campigly and four grandchildren.

I. B. Benedict is ready to meet the 21st Century with a solid group of highly trained managers motivated to outperform the competition with proven methods.

COLLINS ELECTRICAL COMPANY INC.

In 1924 W. J. Collins, the company founder, hired one man, electrician A. J. "Gus" Sanguinetti. In 1927 Collins turned fifty percent of the business over to Sanguinetti in return for a debt of $2,499.00 in unpaid wages and within two years the electrician had sole ownership of the company. The annual gross income was $2,000.00 and assets included one Model T Ford, a Dodge Truck and an Overland business/pleasure automobile. He hired four men and organized a business team.

Sanguinetti's first major projects were State Hospitals in Stockton and Mendocino. "Gus" wanted workers to do quality jobs. Employees soon learned that he tolerated nothing but the best. He wanted men who were willing to grow with the company. In 1955 he hired 16 year old John Nomellini. "Gus" put him to work doing odd office jobs a full year, before he was allowed to apprentice in the shop.

The company needed a bookkeeper, so "Gus" called the Business Department at Stockton High School. He asked about the best student in the bookkeeping class. It turned out to be Henning Thompson, age 19. He was hired straight out of high school, as the company bookkeeper.

When World War II broke out, both Nomellini and Thompson went into military service. Sanguinetti recognized they were his best men and he made a promise. When they returned he would make them part owners in the company. He kept his promise, but in the mean time there was war generated business at hand.

The company's first out-of-state job was for the U. S. Army in Lovelock, Nevada It was just the beginning of sub-contract jobs on vital military installations. The Camp Parks project came to an approximate total cost of $2,600,000.

In 1946 Collins joined the National Electrical Contractors Association (N. E. C. A.) and incorporated as the Collins Electrical Company in 1949.

Sumiden Wire Products.

Acme Electric of Reno, Nevada joined Collins in some projects. Two years later the companies joined as Acme-Collins and operated thus for 50 years until it dropped the Acme name. Al Schwall who had started in the Stockton shop in 1937 was named co-manager with Roy Di-Pietro. The latter was the first and last employee of that branch until the name of Acme was dropped. The Reno Branch completed many big jobs including military installations, high-rise Reno hotels, etc.

During the Korean War the Stockton office organized a marine division that did sub-contract work under Stockton's Colberg Boat Works, a U. S. Navy contractor. A Sacramento Branch was opened with the purchase of Mapes Electric. Carroll Keys, a Stockton native became branch manager in 1958.

Their largest project was $6,100,000 for the State Archives Building.

A Merced Branch was opened in 1953 to handle work at the Castle Air Force Base. Another branch was opened in Modesto. Four years later another was added in Marina near Monterey. That division worked on numerous projects including Fort Ord Barracks and the Aquarium at Monterey.

In 1958 Collin's Electrical Company celebrated its 30th year with a volume of $8,000,000. The company continued to expand buying Modern Electric of Fresno. Operations also moved into San Francisco as Wright/Collins Electric. This branch also proved productive with a wide variety of projects. Their last big job was at Skywalker Studio for George Lucas.

A pole line job was completed in Oregon in 1961. This was not the first or last electrical transmission or generating jobs. Projects were completed at San Francisco's Cherry Power House, Hover Dam's #2 generator and additional line jobs. Collins Electrical Co. of San Francisco was organized in 1965, with George Clyne as a partner/manager. Their projects included; the Alcoa Building, Hunters Point Naval Shipyard, Bank of American Computer Center and Levi Plaza.

Sanguinetti did not get to see these projects completed, as he had a heart attack and died November 6, 1966. He had set the company on course by nurturing his best employees. His philosophy of settling only for the best was ingrained. He had honored his promise to Nomellini and Thompson and made them part owners of the company. They were ready to carry on the tradition. John Nomellini, hired at the age of 16, became president and Henning Thompson, hired at age 19, was named secretary/treasurer.

The company business did not slow, it moved on. In 1970 *Engineering New Record* Magazine named Collin's as one of the top ten electrical companies in the nation. The Sacramento branch undertook a project for the Chico State University, Butte College and the Calaveras Cement plant in Redding. The corporation received two U. S. Navy awards of Merit for Government projects. Company officers challenged and won a legal decision on a questionable State tax system and were rewarded with a rebate check of $140,000.

The Nomellini/Thompson team worked extremely well. Each in his own area, operations and financial respectively, but each supported the other. Mike Thompson, Henning's son graduated from Arizona State University. He came to the company bookkeeping department and was responsible for converting the department to computers. The company was now into the second generation.

John Nomellini retired in 1983 after 50 years. He is still Honorary Chairman of the Board and, as one employee noted, "Father Confessor." Henning Thompson became the next company president. Both men lived the American dream, starting with the company as teenagers. Carroll Keys became secretary/treasurer. Thompson led him as he had been led by "Gus" Sanguinetti.

Unfortunately Thompson died in 1987 after 50 years of service. His former understudy, Carroll Keys, became the first president not on the early team. Eugene "Gene" Gini became senior vice president. The latter had been a reservist in the Army Corps of Engineers, where he trained as an electrician and lineman. Although he did not intend to continue in the field, a member of his and the Nomellini family arranged an interview with John. Even though

University of the Pacific Burns Tower.

San Joaquin County Human Services Building.

he was a third cousin, Nomellini considered him family and hired him as a shop boy in 1960.

Within six months Gini was in charge of repairing, tagging, logging and distributing tools to other branches. He served his time as an apprentice and became a journeyman, foreman, Modesto branch manager and finally president of the company. Ray Quitiquit became Modesto manager. Gini's wife is the Modesto office manager and son Brian will become branch manager when Quitiquit retires at the end of 1998. Gini's son, Kevin, is manager of the Sacramento branch and was named one of Sacramento's top 20 managers in 1998.

Family concern is extended to all employees. Safety was always a major concern, but accident rates grew as the number of employees grew. When 75 accidents occurred in 1990-91, new safety programs were initiated. Both protective eye glasses and back braces became requirements. The next year accidents dropped to 35 and the following year to only nine. Road crews, who work under the most hazardous conditions, receive special training and have drastically cut accident rates. Job

foremen receive recognition for accident free jobs. The crew on a Fresno school job clocked 27,000 accident free man hours. Both employees and the company have benefited.

Employee longevity is astonishing. One fourth of all employees have served 20 years and those with 10 years and more have clocked over 1,589 man-years of service. Thirty employees have worked for 30 years and ten for 35 years. The original team of three, contributed 150 years. Bill Harmon worked for the company for 53 years and was senior estimator when he retired. Royce Mayo, Stockton branch manager since 1990, has lasted 41 years and is known in Stockton as "Mr. Collins Electric" for his service to both customers and community. One of the company officers noted, "If you want a job done, call Royce."

The current board of directors consists of Gene Gini, president Larry L. Schlenker, vice president and Charles E. Plaster, secretary/treasurer. Schlenker started with the company in 1961. He typed invoices, statements and did odd jobs in the accounting department long before he became the purchasing agent.

As vice president he oversees purchasing, contract administration, submittal coordination and supply lead time. His son, Steven, is a journeyman electrician for the company.

Charles Plaster aimed for a career in the electrical business. He trained at Modesto Jr. College and went to work in Los Angeles before moving to Collins in 1968. As secretary/treasurer, he is responsible for the estimating department and participates in project management for the Stockton unit. His son David is a 20 year employee and currently a project manager in the Stockton operation.

As far as the company is concerned, Gini sees the fastest growing areas in Northern California as Stockton, first, Sacramento, second and Modesto third. The company has from 250 to 350 employees, depending on current projects. The annual income is $45,000,000.00. Over the past 74 years the company has been a major contributor to the economic health of Stockton and other communities in which it operates.

COMPUTERLAND OF STOCKTON

An industry pioneer since 1976, ComputerLand of Stockton can claim a stability unique in an industry where accelerating change is the only constant. ComputerLand was the first dealer to sell personal computers from IBM PC, and the first to sell Hewlett-Packard, Compaq and other industry leaders.

In January 1992, Elias Boudames purchased the ComputerLand franchise store. Over the years, the store has evolved from a PC retailer to high-end systems integrators, serving the demand of local businesses. Services include networking and system integration solutions, training services in their training facility, technology staffing services, disaster relief equipment and facilities.

Above
Computerland retail store.

Left
Computerland corporate store in the California Building downtown.

Computerland's success story is founded on their relationships with business customers. They have customers that have been with them since the beginning of their operation.

They are most proud of their ComputerLand site in downtown Stockton. The California Building will serve as a base for future expansion and as a magnet to related computer firms such as programming, web development and vertical applications. The California Building is comprised of a nine-story, quality commercial building, constructed in 1917. It was built for Farmers and Merchant Bank. The ground floor and lobby include marble floors and vaulted ceilings with ornate painted plaster. Upper floors typically include marble wainscot and stained wood ceilings.

ComputerLand is also very excited about their new on-line store at www.clandstore.com. Customers can custom-configure their computers and order them over a secure site on the Internet. The configuration will get assembled within 24 hours and be delivered to their customers.

Elias Boudames says: "We look forward to serving the business computing needs of our community for many years to come."

CUSTOM FOOD MACHINERY, INC.

Custom Food Machinery, Inc., which displays its gargantuan collection of used food-processing equipment in an East Market Street showcase so large that customers do their shopping in golf carts, had its decidedly modest origins in confines so small that workshop, storage area and showroom combined to fit into Ron McNiel Sr.'s residential garage in Watsonville, California.

Mr. McNiel learned the trade from his father Nick Jozovich, a Yugoslavian emigrant, who began manufacturing food processing equipment in San Jose in

McNiel accumulated such a large and diverse inventory that he was able to set up more than 30 complete factories to process fruits and vegetables in countries as scattered as Greece, Bulgaria, Yugoslavia and Mexico.

To satisfy his need for space, in 1973 McNiel rented the old Duffy Mott plant in San Jose, and his clientele continued to balloon to include the giants of food processing: Del-Monte, Stokley, H.J. Heinz, Pillsbury, Seneca-Green Giant, Nestle, Hunt Wesson, Nabisco, Tri-Valley Growers, American

unchallenged as the world's largest supplier of used and rebuilt food-processing, packaging and can-making equipment.

CFM offers its customers a catalogue of services. It will simply purchase available equipment from a single machine to an entire factory to maintain its inventory of 10,000-plus items, or it will locate special items when customers seek specific brands, models, and sizes of snippers, bag sealers, scales, blenders, labelers, peelers or any other common or specialized machine. Under its Asset Recovery Program, the company acts as an agent allowing clients to sell surplus, obsolete, retired or even on-line and working equipment either as is, reconditioned or totally rebuilt under its nine-point rebuilding program, which meets standards as demanding as those of the original manufacturers. The seller can chose to have CFM inventory the equipment and leave it on site or display the equipment in CFM's sales facilities in Stockton or Bailey, Michigan. Because of the knowledge and the enormous number of contacts they have accumulated over the years, the CFM sales force can guarantee that sellers will get the maximum value from their used equipment, and after the sales are complete, clients have the option of having CFM deposit the income in a trade account for use in purchasing goods, services or equipment.

Custom Food Machinery and Delta Management headquarters at the Waterfront Warehouse overlooking the Stockton Yacht Harbor.

1947. Beginning in 1955, Mr. Jozovich—assisted by Ron and his brother Richard—shifted his focus to rebuilding equipment for local food processors such as Hunt Foods and Gerber Baby Products, and after the father sold his company in 1969, the son formed Custom Food Machinery, Inc., to continue the familiar business of selling used and rebuilt food-processing equipment.

During the 1970s, CFM expanded its markets throughout the state and the nation, into Canada and Mexico, and eventually into every region of the world.

National Can, the Ball Corporation, Silgan Containers, Crown Cork & Seal, and General Foods. A decade later he purchased the former Stokely Van Camp plant across the street in San Jose, but even then CFM lacked sufficient display space as it grew to dominate the *World Market* in used and rebuilt food-processing equipment.

CFM moved into the 20-acre East Market Street rebuilding-warehousing-displaying complex in 1992, added a can-making division in 1993 that now controls more than 70% of the worldwide market for used can-making machinery, currently enjoys a growth rate of 25% annually and reigns

The company keeps a current inventory in its computer system of items in its showrooms or available under the Asset Recovery Program, and each quarter it prints an inventory listing in detail the make, model, condition, reference numbers, age, location and even photographs of machines designed for thousands of operations such as processing sauces, soups and juices; bottling champagne; slicing, cutting, shredding chopping, grinding, coring, pitting, stemming, and extruding fruits and vegetables; cooking produce in kettles ranging in size from five to 25,000 gallons; mixing, blending and sifting

Custom Food Machinery's 20-acre East Market Street rebuilding-warehousing-displaying complex.

baking and cereal products; frying; storing liquids, dry goods, and produce; handling wastewater; freezing and refrigerating; forming meatballs, ravioli, noodles and other pasta ingredients; filling and sealing twelve-ounce and sixteen-ounce cans of beer at a rate of 1,000 per minute.

After selling equipment at a 40% to 70% discount from equivalent new machinery, CFM will assist customers anywhere in the world with installation, on-line adjustments, test runs and a full day of supervision by CFM engineers.

CFM also offers a rebuilding program under which its mechanics keep a customer's machinery in good functioning order, working alongside the client's mechanics if desirable. It has a trade-in program giving allowances for used equipment. It furnishes spare parts, temporarily stripping them from on-hand machines when necessary. And it has in-house auctioneers and arrangements with leading auctioneer firms across the nation to assist customers in liquidation of their equipment and other assets.

Cribbing from 21st century technology, Custom Food Machinery has devised a way to allow potential customers from any spot on the earth to take an electronic "walking" tour of the Stockton display complex, observing any piece of equipment close-up from any angle. Consequently, at any time they choose, those interested in purchasing used food-processing equipment may see available machinery simply by logging onto the CFM website at *www.cfmcan.com*, clicking on "Virtual Tour," and downloading Quicktime and Quicktime VR for Macintosh or Windows. Those who prefer the view from the golf cart can fly in and take advantage of CFM's shuttle service to and from airports in San Francisco, Oakland, and San Jose.

Delta Management, Custom Food Machinery's real estate division, operated by Ron McNiel's stepson Mike Leith, broker of record, leases and manages a number of large facilities formerly used by major processors, including the 153,000 square-foot Tri-Valley Growers and the 272,000 square-foot Banquet plants in Turlock, the Waterfront Warehouse office complex overlooking the Stockton Yacht Harbor—in which CFM maintains its home offices, and the 248,000 square-foot Keystone Foods plant in the town of North East, Pennsylvania.

CFM remains a family enterprise. Vice president Ron McNiel, Jr., joined the firm when he graduated from St. Mary's University in 1989, daughter Lynedt McNiel has worked in the sales department since 1991, and they frequently accompany their father to trade shows around the world, promoting their product as far afield as Orlando and Tampa, Chicago, Venezuela, and Thailand. The McNiels envision continuing prosperity for CFM, encouraged by the certain confidence that food is a commodity not likely to go out of fashion in the foreseeable future, that repeat business from processors such as Del Monte Foods and Tri-Valley Growers testifies to the quality of their service and their rebuilding program, and that they can provide anyone, anywhere, with any piece of food-processing equipment imaginable.

DIAMOND WALNUT GROWERS

From its humble beginnings in 1912 as a small group of visionary farmers to today's position of industry leadership, Diamond Walnut Growers' long history is a testament to innovation, tenacity, and old-fashioned hard work.

Two world wars, the Great Depression, changing demographics, and increasing environmental pressures affected

but true success was not realized until the 1912 formation of the California Walnut Growers Association (CWGA), Diamond's Los Angeles-based predecessor.

CWGA counted numerous "firsts" in the ensuing years: It was first on the scene with a national advertising campaign, with shelled nuts in airtight containers, with individually "branded" nuts.

Act of 1933 and formation of the Walnut Control Board (today's Walnut Marketing Board). By the following year the new marketing agreement had brought a measure of control to the overwhelming surplus.

Once again, the times were characterized by boom and bust. Export markets dried up when conflict in Europe broke out in the late 1930s and declined until the United States declared war in late 1941. The situation was improved by a short crop, a holiday rush of food purchasing, and government purchases of protein-rich walnuts as a meat substitute for the troops. Tin cans were prohibited for the war's duration so shelled walnuts appeared in cellophane bags, yet another Diamond "first."

A legacy of World War II was a tremendous population explosion in Southern California. As housing tracts edged out Southland orchards, growers headed for Central and Northern California. By the late 1940s, these regions accounted for some 70 percent of walnut bearing acreage, and CWGA turned its sights northward in its search for a new home, zeroing in on Stockton, in the heart of the great Central Valley, as the optimum site.

In 1997, Diamond marked its 85th aniversary with a gala celebration, keynoted by President Michael Mendes.

farmers as they did the rest of the nation. Diamond met these and other challenges head on, emerging today as the No. 1 processor and marketer of ingredient nuts, with annual sales surpassing $220 million and a membership of more than 2,000 grower-owners.

Walnuts have long been part of the California landscape, the first trees brought here by the Spanish padres. Commercial plantings took root by the 1880s, but even as cultural techniques improved and plantings increased, early growers were at the mercy of a mercurial marketplace. Several times they attempted to organize cooperatively to bring stability to their fledgling industry,

Membership climbed, thanks to the association's marketplace triumphs and the leadership of such industry pioneers as Charles C. Teague and Carlyle Thorpe. The situation improved further with World War I, which signaled a sharp decline in walnut imports from France, California's primary competitor. By war's end CWGA had made significant inroads which continued through the 1920s, and when the decade closed, the grower-owned marketing cooperative controlled fully 85 percent of the crop.

But the Great Depression spelled potential disaster, exacerbated by large crops of poor quality. Some of the pressure was relieved by sales abroad, but the real answer lay in market regulation for the entire industry, which came with passage of the Agricultural Adjustment

Through the decades, magazine advertising has helped make Diamond "the world's favorite walnut."

A state-of-the-art processing and packaging facility was constructed there and dedicated in 1956. Covering 550,000 square feet on 75 acres, it was and still is the largest and most modern walnut processing plant in the world, receiving as many as 8 million pounds of walnuts a day at the height of harvest. At the same time, CWGA changed its name to link the organization more closely to its brand, officially becoming Diamond Walnut Growers, Inc. Relocated and reenergized, the cooperative actively developed new products and outlets, and years of fantastic growth followed. Diamond walnuts began appearing in many popular convenience foods, while new international markets were forged. As the walnut industry's innovator, Diamond was the first with a co-generation facility that utilized shells, largely a waste product, to generate electricity.

But new threats loomed for the cooperative. These included retaliatory tariffs imposed on U.S. walnuts in the early 1980s, and a depressed economic environment that affected virtually every California commodity. Ripon grower Gerald Barton stepped up to Diamond's presidency, building a strong management team and enhancing the co-op's financial position. New air separation equipment installed in 1986 resulted in a spectacular 200 percent return on investment, while federal and state export marketing programs further spurred international growth for the entire industry.

History refuses to stand still, and the 1990s have posed numerous challenges as well as remarkable opportunities.

Increasingly stringent environmental regulations affect every aspect of growing, processing, and marketing walnuts. At the same time, ongoing genetic research promises exciting breakthroughs in plant breeding and pest resistance. Recent scientific studies have documented nuts' many health attributes, with Diamond and the rest of the industry mounting a long-term marketing strategy to position walnuts as an integral part of a healthy diet.

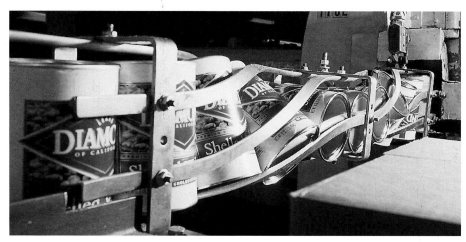

Diamond is the industry leader in processing technology at its modern, state-of-the-art Stockton facility.

With yields on the upswing and plantings on the rise, Diamond is prepared to handle the ever-larger crops of the future. Efforts to broaden the focus of European consumers beyond the traditional inshell to shelled walnuts are bearing fruit, and the company continues to introduce innovative new packs in such key markets as Germany and Italy. Through Diamond's marketing efforts and high-spec capabilities, Japan has emerged in recent years as the No. 1 export market for shelled walnuts.

In 1998, under the leadership of

Each premium walnut was—and still is—individually stamped with a small Diamond brand, a practice which began in earnest with the 1926 season.

President Michael Mendes, Diamond made huge strides toward enhancing its long-term competitive posture and viability. A key is its entry into the "pegboard" market, that section of the baking aisle where small packets of walnuts, almonds, pecans, and other nuts are displayed on hooks. The business is strategically important to Diamond's future direction as a full-line culinary nut supplier.

Diamond's balance sheet remains rock solid, with returns to members exceeding the independent field price in eight of 10 years. The company continues to invest in new research and development to find new ways to add value to walnuts. At the same time, it recognizes the role its work force plays in long-term success and has strengthened its management team and proactively works to attract and retain superior personnel at all levels.

Throughout its long, proud history, the hallmark of Diamond has been value creation. Thanks to its owners—a grower membership second to none—assisted by the most experienced sales, marketing, production, and field personnel in the world, Diamond Walnut Growers remains on the cutting edge, and in a prime position to lead the industry into the 21st century.

DOWNING PAINT & EQUIPMENT COMPANY

John Orville Downing a credit manager for Pacific Gas and Electric Company was transferred to the Stockton Main Office of the company in 1940. He was located at the main office at the corner of California and Channel Streets in Stockton. There was a small paint store down the block which caught his interest. He purchased the business with Carl Brown, a partner, in 1944. Within a couple of years Downing bought out his partner and renamed the company, Downing Paint Company.

He moved the business to the corner of El Dorado and Lindsey Streets. The company supplied all kinds of paint and wall coverings. In 1962 Downing relocated the main store to the corner of Main and Grant Streets. He purchased the building to the immediate south and utilized it as a warehouse for the growing business. Outlets were opened on Pacific Avenue and eventually Lincoln Center.

Both Downing's wife, Edna and daughter Suedee Wolfe were doing the accounting for the business in 1977 when Wolfe's husband died. The following year, 1978, Orville Downing died leaving his wife and daughter to run the business. The two women ran the business alone for seven years.

The accounting department was still located in a north Stockton store, but

Corporate headquarters in Stockton.

when computers came into use the department was moved to the main store. Suedee's son, Randy Wolfe, graduated from college and went into the business doing outside sales. In 1985 Suedee married Carl Howell, a salesman for an automotive distribution company. Carl and Randy both moved into the management of the company.

From the beginning, the company had sold a wide variety of paint and wallcoverings and had moved into north Stockton to be closer to customers. When automotive paint became the dominant factor in the business, the company closed the other outlets and concentrated on automotive paints. In

Pictured front left; Edna Downing, founder of the company along with husband (Orville Downing deceased), Suedee Howell also in front row, back row; left to right, Randy Wolfe, Carl Howell, Bryan Colyer and Julie Colyer.

1988 they opened an automotive paint store in Fairfield, followed by others in Lodi, Sonora and Modesto. They moved into the current corporation headquarters, the former warehouse on Grant Street, in 1993.

The industry has evolved from brush painting to the use of high volume low pressure spray guns which are environmentally friendly. Colors have gone from only a few standard colors to over 100,000 different ones today. Today's paints include single stage to tri stage systems utilizing high tech, Poly Urethane clear coats. The company uses a sophisticated computer (Spectro-photometer) "Color Eye" to match colors. The computer looks at a sample and produces a formula to create a matching color.

This is a family run business with Edna Downing acting as chairman of the board. Her daughter, Suedee Howell is president, her son, Randy Wolfe, is vice president and daughter Julie Colyer is secretary/treasurer. Suedee's husband, Carl Howell is the C.E.O.. Julie's husband Bryan Colyer does industrial sales for the Company.

With a recent reorganization of the corporation and 40 employees, Downing Paint company is ready for the 21st Century.

THE GREATER STOCKTON CHAMBER OF COMMERCE

In 1901, three public-spirited Stockton citizens—attorney Oscar Parkinson, superintendent of schools James Barr and county treasurer W. C. Neumiller—took the initial steps to organize a Stockton Chamber of Commerce.

In its inception, the agency was created to promote the growth, prosperity and development of the City of Stockton. Now the "Greater" Stockton Chamber of Commerce, the mission continues to be to "aggressively develop and promote an economically vibrant business community."

The Chamber is a member of the California Chamber of Commerce, and has been accredited with the United States Chamber of Commerce since 1977. Since the 1980s, the role of the Chamber has shifted from community promotion to business advocacy. Currently, the Chamber focuses on helping each of its 1400 plus members build and promote their business through exposure and education, discounting business services and working to affect the future business environment and workforce.

Currently, as in the past, the Chamber provides programs that develop future leaders and encourage business and education to form partnerships. The first project of the newly formed Chamber in 1901 was the endorsement of a $150,000 bond issue for the erection of the old

Stockton Ag Expo attendees enjoy a 23 year old tradition at the first Ag Show in the west each January.

Stockton High School. Other historical efforts include advocating a San Joaquin River deep-water channel and the Port of Stockton, California's first inland seaport; urging the establishment of Stockton Metropolitan Airport; and supporting a Stockton-East San Joaquin Water District. Among current programs specifically directed toward improving future leaders is Leadership Stockton, which has promoted and fostered the development of leaders in the greater Stockton area for over 17 years.

Presently under the leadership of Chief Executive Officer Paula McCloskey, the Chamber has a long history of fine leadership and an aggressive approach to government affairs. Noteworthy key projects include establishing the Private Industry Council for job training and placement; working for passage of Measure K, which increased sales tax for county transportation projects; advocat-

ing to keep the 209 area code in San Joaquin County and pushing to complete the crosstown freeway. Current Chamber projects include downtown revitalization, reducing government red tape and quality of life issues.

A number of committees have been formed by the Chamber to advocate for the special interests of business. The Government Relations Council helps business succeed by improving the regulatory and legislative environment; the Manufacturers Industrial Roundtable provides and promotes programs and opportunities for manufacturing and industry members; and the Small Business Council provides training and advocacy for small-to-medium-sized businesses.

In addition, special events to help expose and promote business are held throughout the year, including Stockton Ag Expo, Chamber Night at the Ports, the Athena Award and the Annual Golf Tournament. In 1998, the Chamber teamed up with community leaders and volunteers to help bring the spirit of the early gold rush settlers back to Stockton, with the San Francisco 49ers beginning the first of ten seasons of summer training at the University of the Pacific.

The Greater Stockton Chamber of Commerce has positioned itself as a voice for business, and continues to encourage its members to "put us to work for you."

Stockton Chamber is recognized statewide for their business advocacy program. Martha Shaver receiving award from Assemblyman Michael Machado.

GUNTERT & ZIMMERMAN

Guntert & Zimmerman was founded as Hickinbotham Bros. Construction Division by the late Ronald M. Guntert, Sr., in 1942. His was a classic American success story where the son of a Swiss-German immigrant sea captain saw an opportunity, worked hard, overcame adversity and started a business at the outbreak of WWII. By the end of the war, he was building tank lighters, tugs, 60 ton floating cranes and 176 foot inter-island supply vessels for the military. Hickinbotham Bros. was awarded the Army "E" for excellence in quality and workmanship. Ronald Guntert was proud of the fact that his little shipyard (almost 600 employees during the war) had more craftsmen than the entire Mare Island Shipyard. He prided himself on their innovativeness. Moreover, he had the drive to push and promote a good idea to acceptance.

Guntert & Zimmerman started building heavy construction machinery beginning right after the end of the war when the military work dried up. Ronald Guntert's experience in building gold dredges and the severe duty they were subjected to, coupled with Zimmerman's first hand

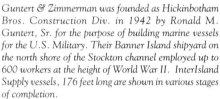

Guntert & Zimmerman was founded as Hickinbotham Bros. Construction Div. in 1942 by Ronald M. Guntert, Sr. for the purpose of building marine vessels for the U.S. Military. Their Banner Island shipyard on the north shore of the Stockton channel employed up to 600 workers at the height of World War II. InterIsland Supply vessels, 176 feet long are shown in various stages of completion.

experience as the master mechanic on the first set of automated canal trimming and concrete lining machines built by Clyde Wood, led them to the huge public works projects of the late 40s. In 1948, Guntert & Zimmerman designed and built the first successful canal construction machines used in the western United States which included a rail mounted slipform. These behemoth machines weighed in the neighborhood of 150 tons each. The first canal liners, which were slipforms, ran on rails. The first crawler track mounted canal slipform was successfully demonstrated

by G&Z in 1956. These canal machines were also equipped with automatic line and grade control systems.

In 1956, G&Z demonstrated the concrete slipform paving technique for highways to the California Department of Transportation while paving the bottom of the Los Angeles River, an Army Corp of Engineers Project. G&Z had been paving at 60 feet wide. For the purposes of the demonstration, the machine was knocked down to 24 feet. Later that year, Teichert Construction and Guntert & Zimmerman used a 24 foot wide G&Z Slipform on a section of Highway 99 south of Stockton, California. The use of the slipform didn't gain wide acceptance until 1959. The Guntert & Zimmerman Slipform Paver wasn't the first slipform, but it was the first successful slipform used on a highway. Its patented line and grade control system and weight allowed it to meet California's seven inch per mile profilograph specification in 1959.

One of the earliest G&Z bucketline canal trimmers used to build the Delta Mendota canal in California's Central Valley in 1948. A canal liner (not shown) follows the trimmer and lines the canal with concrete.

Today, Guntert & Zimmerman sets the standard in Highway and Airport Paving machinery. Their machines were successfully used to pave all of the concrete runways, taxiways and aprons on the Dallas Ft. Worth Airport. Much of this airport paving was paved at 50' wide. Guntert & Zimmerman Slipforms were also used on Atlanta International Airport, Ross Perot Alliance Airport, Los Angeles International and most recently the new Denver International Airport (DIA).

One of the many steel processing tools at Guntert & Zimmerman's new Ripon facility. Truck trailer body parts are shown being rolled for a Guntert Steel customer.

On the highway front, G&Z's introduction of the first successful slipform mounted Dowel Bar Inserter to the United States in 1987, forever changed the way roads would be built in the United States. The mechanical Dowel Bar Inserter eliminates the need for the supporting dowel basket and the crew required to install them on the transverse contraction joints. G&Z has successfully introduced their patented mechanical Dowel Bar Insertion into the States of Pennsylvania, Wisconsin, Texas, Delaware, Colorado, Nevada, Louisiana, Mississippi, Minnesota and Illinois.

In 1948, Guntert & Zimmerman formed a steel supply division, which was called Guntert & Zimmerman Sales

Guntert & Zimmerman bucketline trimmer, one of ten machines recently delivered to Pakistan for use on a huge hydroelectric power scheme on the Indus River. This machine was designed and built by G & Z and weighed almost 200 tons.

Div., Inc. L. R. Zimmerman's shares in both companies were purchased by Guntert in 1956. The supply division changed its name to Guntert Sales Div., Inc. in 1961, and it is more commonly known today as Guntert Steel.

Guntert Steel services Stockton's and central California's steel and steel processing needs with personalized service and a readily available supply of steel sheet, plate and bar stock. Prompt processing and delivery of services such as steel sawing, shearing, forming, burning and punching are how Guntert

Guntert & Zimmerman S850 Slipform Paver being used on an interstate concrtete highway project near Chestes, Arkansas.

Steel continues to prosper in today's competitive market.

Both corporations shared the seven acre waterfront facility on Banner Island in Stockton until 1984 when the two corporations relocated 26 miles south to Ripon, California. This new facility is situated along Highway 99 on 22 acres, of which 13 acres are available for future expansion.

KROLOFF, BELCHER, SMART, PERRY & CHRISTOPHERSON

Yale S. Kroloff—abandoning the security of an in-house position with Farmer's Insurance Company in Oakland, California—established a private practice with Jack Miller in downtown Stockton's Esquire Theater Building on Main Street in August, 1946. Mr. Kroloff continued to represent Farmer's Insurance, maintaining a relationship which continued for over forty years. In 1952, Richard Belcher joined the prospering firm. Creighton University educated Kroloff and Hastings trained Belcher were a study in contrasts: Kroloff was ambitious, flamboyant, and dapper while Belcher

Yale Kroloff, founder of the firm.

was gracious, soft-spoken, and well mannered. The combination of their diversified strengths and abilities helped develop one of the most successful firms in San Joaquin County.

After Claude H. Smart, Jr. joined the firm in 1955, and Thomas O. Perry and Gary Christopherson became partners in August, 1975, the firm became known as Kroloff, Belcher, Smart, Perry & Christopherson. Richard Belcher retired from the firm in 1980; and though Yale Kroloff retired about the same time, he continued to don his three-piece suits and visit his elegant wood-paneled office almost daily.

In 1952, the firm moved to 1106 N. El Dorado Street, and in 1971, to 1044 N. El Dorado Street, where the practice was headquartered for over seventeen years. In 1988, the partnership moved to a 22,900 square foot brick office building at 7540 Shoreline Drive.

At one time involved primarily in insurance defense, the firm, now one of the largest in San Joaquin County, includes lawyers who practice in the following areas:

- Business and commercial law, including entity formation, dissolution, and transactions
- Civil litigation
- Defense of hospitals and doctors in medical malpractice actions
- Employment and labor law counseling and litigation
- Estate planning, trust, and probate law
- Health Care law
- Insurance law and defense
- Personal injury litigation
- Real estate transactions and litigation

Yale Kroloff and Richard Belcher were Fellows of the American College of Trial Lawyers. Current partners include members of the American Board of Trial Advocates, a State Bar of California certified specialist in estate planning, trust, and probate law, and members of national bar specialty organizations.

The current offices at 7540 Shoreline Drive.

Richard Belcher, who joined the firm in 1952.

The present partners contribute their time and talents to many professional, community service, and charitable organizations, including local, state, and national bar associations, local public agencies and committees, the University of Pacific Business School, San Joaquin County Historical Society & Museum, Dameron Hospital Foundation, St. Joseph's Hospital Medical Center, the Salvation Army, the American Heart Association, Big Brothers and Sisters of San Joaquin County, the Yosemite Club, the Chamber of Commerce, and several local Rotary clubs.

They also regularly write articles and present seminars to local and state bar and community organizations on legal topics.

MEDIAONE

On May 13, 1997, a new kind of company was launched in Stockton and across the country. Continental Cablevision, which had served Stockton and the surrounding area with cable television since 1969, became MediaOne, a Broadband telecommunications company. In a time of rapid evolution, MediaOne's fully interactive two-way Broadband networks will enable the company to deliver superior entertainment, communications and information services for the home of today and tomorrow.

In addition to the city of Stockton, the Stockton headquarters serves Lodi, Manteca, Lathrop, San Joaquin County, Calaveras County and Amador County, with a total of 94,000 homes subscribing. MediaOne employs more than 250 associates in the areas of customer service, advertising, installation, construction, dispatch, marketing, sales, human resources, training, engineering, community and government affairs, and business services. Operations offices have been located on Tam O'Shanter Drive since 1984, with a regional administrative and associate training center that serves northern California and Nevada housed on Deer Park Drive.

MediaOne is best known for its high quality video programming. One of the unique aspects of MediaOne is its Community Programming, which presents both locally-oriented programs produced by MediaOne, and community access programs produced by local citizens to reflect a wide range of interests. MediaOne also makes available a channel for local government and a channel for education. The Community Bulletin Board acquaints viewers with many events presented by community groups and organizations, and provides free public service announcements.

MediaOne is proud of its commitment to education. "Cable in the Classroom" is a program that enables teachers to access a wide range of programming that enriches the curriculum. It provides quality commercial-free educational programs that

teachers can use to enhance and enliven learning. The service is provided at no cost to schools. Each school also receives a free cable hookup.

MediaOne has made a commitment to provide free, high speed Internet access to California elementary and secondary schools, both public and private, in its service district within a year of offering the service commercially to customers within the community

Serving the community is important to MediaOne, which knows the value of being a good neighbor and contributing to the quality of life. It supports many local events and is a major contributer to community organizations.

MediaOne advocates volunteerism among its associates, and sponsors a program called COOL–Community

A fiberoptic technician checks optical power at an amplifier node in the Stockton system.

Homework Hotline is a public service program of MediaOne. Co-sponsored by the San Joaquin County Office of Education, this popular program provides an opportunity for students and parents to call in homework questions and receive help from a certified teacher.

Outreach and Online Learning. This program encourages MediaOne associates to adopt an elementary or secondary school classroom and provide volunteer assistance to teachers and students. MediaOne recognizes the volunteer effort with a payment to each school of up to $600 per associate. Additionally, the company will match dollar for dollar any MediaOne associate's donation made to schools or non-profit organizations.

Today, MediaOne is at the forefront of high-capacity, Broadband service providers, offering top-quality multichannel video services, and the ongoing deployment of new technology-based services. Building on its Continental Cablevision heritage and sterling reputation, MediaOne is community-driven and committed to providing the highest quality cable television services. As an innovative communications company, MediaOne delivers the most sophisticated interactive, multimedia products and services available.

The Port of Stockton, circa 1935.

PORT OF STOCKTON

Nineteen seventy-seven marks a milestone; it is the beginning of the modern history of the Port of Stockton. Alexander Krygsman becomes Port Director and brings a new era of success to a port, which was, to put it mildly, in a rut. "Lex," as he likes to be called, took on the responsibility of turning around the fortune of a facility which for almost a decade had degenerated into hard times and was plagued by enormous financial losses. Turning the Port around and keeping it growing for 20 years is the result of his dedication, hard work, adaptability to change and his ability to inspire his staff to emulate those qualities.

Gold Fever! Like many other river ports and harbors, Stockton was little more than a trading post in the middle of nowhere. Then in 1848, at a nearby sawmill owned by John Sutter, the discovery of gold and the ensuing gold rush of 1849 forever changed the face of America, and with it the fortunes of the Port of Stockton. The gold rush may have put Stockton on the map, but then the gold fields started to fizzle

Port Director Alexander Krygsman.

out, and so did the fortunes of the Port. After the boom, the Civil War, the Transcontinental Railroad and Manifest Destiny; the movement to create a nation that reached, "From Sea to Shining Sea," diverted attention from the need for a deep water port. The rapid build-up and despoilment of the land severely impacted the river with silting to the point that navigation was severely limited.

By the late 1860s, Stockton, the San Joaquin River, its Delta and the fertile San Joaquin Valley became the most productive farming region in the world. Little attention was paid to the Port or its condition until the 1870s, when farmers and businessmen started to become aware of the need for economical transportation. A plan was conceived for a canal to link Stockton directly to the deep water of the San Joaquin. This plan languished for several reasons: lack of capital, economic downturns, floods, and political pressure from other commu-

nities. Other obstacles also surfaced: the need for irrigation, hydro-electric power dams, hydraulic mining, and potable water, along with sportsmen, all competing for the same water that was needed to provide deep water navigation. The idea, however, did not go away.

Despite the lack of direct deep-sea shipping, Stockton continued to develop. Stockton was virtually in the middle of the population and economic expansion of California. Overland transportation, both road and rail, developed in and around Stockton. Stockton was an important transportation center which channeled the riches of agriculture into a worldwide distribution network. Water transportation remained limited, and despite a dramatic leap in agricultural production, water carriage of goods remained static. Railroads proliferated and, in an effort to protect their business, were often adversarial to a deep water port. Another factor was the changing markets. The Valley initially was virtually dedicated to wheat, the Great Plains quickly took to wheat farming and the Valley shifted to other more valuable grains—row crops and fruit.

During the first decade of the Twentieth Century, the Port was successful in achieving a 9 foot deep, 200 foot wide channel that brought its viability at least up to the point it had been during the 1850s.

Even the opening of the Panama Canal, which rekindled interest in direct ocean access, and although shipping between the East Coast, Europe and California was rapidly growing, there were few port improvements after 1913. As time progressed the idea and need was always there but, because of constantly changing markets and politics, it was difficult to articulate or justify changing the status quo. Proponents were to constantly reevaluate and redesign the project. The need never went away, the idea never died.

Those who championed the deep water port would ebb and flow until 1927. The Port would remain the domain of riverboats until further improvements were made. In the meantime, the potential for severely limiting future expansion came in the form of proposals for the construction of bridges that could choke off Stockton from the sea. Fortunately, Stockton prevailed, and sufficient vertical and horizontal clearances to accommodate ocean going vessels was engineered into the bridges. This bit of foresight would insure the Port's viability as an inland ocean port. It is evident that even though there was little physical progress, the idea was kept alive. During this period, land was purchased, rights of ways acquired, and plans were developed and constantly refined. Construction of docks and warehouses began.

The morning of February 2, 1933, signaled the official "grand opening" of the Port of Stockton as an international gateway. The deep water port became the on-ramp to the silent liquid highway of world trade. The SS Daisy Gray arrived on that day, first oceangoing vessel to call at the new Port. This was a day of triumph! The whole city celebrated the birth of what was to be known as the "Sunrise Port."

The intervening years saw the fortunes of the Port rise and fall

The modern Port of Stockton.

several times. External factors of local and international politics, changes in industry and general economic conditions would constantly change the way the Port had to do business. The old side-wheeler paddle driven riverboats would fade from the river. World War II would see the Port bustle with activity. Liberty ships were quickly dispatched with supplies to support the Pacific Theater. The Korean War ensued and again the Port of Stockton was pivotal in maintaining the vital supply lines.

After the wars, prosperity continued at the Port through the 1950s. The nation was at peace, there was a

tremendous feeling of national pride. As a nation we could do anything, and nowhere else on the planet was that feeling being manifested more than in California. The automobile was the key to mobility and freedom, in addition to the California Freeways, the Federal Government was embarking on the Interstate Highway Network. The Interstates would link the entire nation with high-speed limited access roads that would speed goods from every American city to the entire nation and the world. California was a magnet for growth.

There was a dark-side to this vast economic expansion. Because business was good and labor plentiful, there was shortsightedness at many ports. Other nations were now competing with us. The new plants, technologies and labor "partnerships" would begin to eclipse our older ways of doing business. The Vietnam War would mask these deficiencies by again forcing supplies and equipment through our nation's port system.

In the 1970s, things changed rapidly. General cargo was becoming the dinosaur of the maritime industry. Cargo was being packed in containers at the factory and loaded directly onto ships. Large self-trimming bulk carriers foreclosed the need for bagged cargo. Change was every-

where, and in a short period of time ports that did not have the foresight to deal with change were quickly relegated to minor players, some ports completely vanished.

The Port of Stockton was no exception. All around the country, port commissioners and their directors scrambled to make sense of what was happening. What once was the economic engine of cities and towns was becoming a nightmare. Various solutions were formulated from vast capital outlays to outright abandonment. Some ports, like Stockton, simply stuck their heads in the ground. Mismanagement, outdated labor practices, non-competitive tariffs, and chasing cargoes that simply didn't exist was the order of the day. The Port languished without direction until the commissioners recruited "Lex" Krygsman.

Upon his arrival, Krygsman knew he had the staff plus the physical assets and basic infrastructure to rebuild the Port. His first order of business was to initiate the deepening of the Channel to a minimum operating draft of 35 feet. This ambitious project took over 10 years to accomplish, but the perseverance of the staff finally prevailed. On May 29, 1987, "37 Feet to The Sea," declared the headlines, as a public

dedication ceremony marked the newly dredged Deep Water Channel. The Port could now compete, it was now economically feasible to load cargo at the Port of Stockton. Also, in order to make the Port a player in the arena of international trade, the Port would require the right cargo handling equipment. Almost immediately Krygsman purchased a variety of machinery, conveyers, and, most importantly, the first of three multi-purpose bridge cranes. These cranes handle a variety of cargo, from containers and project cargo to bulk and general cargo. By being flexible, the Port continues to be insulated from the constant changes inherent to international markets. This wisdom proved itself over the years as the cycle of a given commodity would decline, and another would take its place.

Krygsman's legacy is evident throughout the Port facility. His foresight has enabled the Port to grow and "roll with the punches" as cargoes change. If nothing else is learned from his tenure it is that change is inevitable. As we approach the new millenium, the Port is again looking to deepen the draft of the Channel, acquire additional land for increased volume and expand in other "non-traditional" areas that can enhance the Port's competitive stature.

FACTS ABOUT THE PORT:

Location:	*75 Nautical miles due east of the Golden Gate Bridge*
Berthing:	*Up to 10 ocean cargo ships with a water depth of 40 feet at dockside*
Vessels:	*Up to 900 feet LOA, no beam restrictions*
	Largest ship to call: M/V "El Pampero" - 75,485 DWT - 793 FT LOA
	Largest vessel cargo: M/V "Kyuko" - 38,920 Short Tons
Cranes:	*3 - 30 Ton Bridge Cranes adaptable to a wide variety of cargoes*
Rail Service:	*Union Pacific and Burlington Northern Sante Fe*
Warehousing:	*Over 2.5 million square feet*
Highways:	*1 Mile from I-5 and all major connecting highway systems*

MOUNTAIN VALLEY EXPRESS CO., INC.

Mountain Valley Express is a general commodities, less-than-truck-load (LTL) carrier specializing in overnight delivery service in most of California. Founded in 1976 by Charles L. Giles with one small truck and Dana Corporation, as their major account, the company reached first year revenues of $200,000. By 1980, the firm moved to new corporate headquarters and a terminal in Manteca, California, with revenues reaching $1,000,000.

Service is overnight to 90% of the population of California. Through established and reliable connecting carriers, 99% of all points not served direct by Mountain Valley are second day service. These carriers honor the company's rates and charges and have been selected for their commitment to consistent service. The firm is also certified to handle all hazardous material except Class A and B explosives and poisons. On-going training of employees ensures compliance with California and D.O.T. regulations in the proper handling and transport of hazardous materials.

Mountain Valley Express has elected to remain a "niche" market carrier, serving the special needs of California shippers and receivers in the LTL market. The focus has allowed them to grow methodically so their commitments to customers does not

Mountain Valley headquarters.

exceed their ability to service. Conservative financial management and planning insure their future place in the industry.

The firm emphasizes safety and maintenance as a priority making service commitments to the shipping public. Mountain View proudly points to placing second in their division in 1990 and 1992 and first in 1993, 1994, 1995 and 1996 in the California Trucking Association (CTA) Fleet Safety Awards Programs. Companies are judged on specific performance, including accident frequency, personnel, hiring systems, safety policies and procedures, drivers training, internal accident handling procedures and participation in CTA safety activities. CTA represents trucking companies carrying more than 80% of everything made, grown or sold in California.

Their fleet is maintained through strategically placed company owned full service maintenance facilities in Northern, Central Coastal and Southern California. Since there are occasions when Charles Giles, president and founder, may climb into the drivers seat, you can bet highly skilled and experienced personnel keep this equipment clean and in good repair. Scott Blevins joined the company as director of maintenance in 1983, Don Smith as vice president-director of operations and Dick McIntosh as vice president-

chief financial officer and director of traffic both in 1986, and Betty Moss as director of sales in 1992.

In 1991, a long term continuing relationship was established with New United Motor Manufacturing (NUMMI), a joint venture of General Motors and Toyota, Just-in-time (JIT) which is the basis for this mutually beneficial program operating with a dedicated fleet.

December 1994 marked the joining of Mountain Valley Express and Golden West to improve service opportunities for customers on the Central Coast. The firm now employs in excess of 200 employees, owns 300 pieces of equipment and sales are expected to exceed $12 million.

In 1995 Mountain Valley moved into a new corporate facility and terminal in Manteca, California, followed in 1996 by moving their Southern California hub, first opened in 1988, to a larger facility in Paramount, California. In 1997, a terminal opened in Visalia, California to enhance service in the Madera to Bakersfield areas.

Mountain Valley Express's dedication to customer and community is evidenced through participation in Boys & Girls Clubs; St. Dominic's Hospital; Food Partnership (delivering food free to hungry Californians); and many communities represented by their employees.

THE RECORD

A *Record* newswriter once wrote, "In the beginning was a printer...He handwrote the copy, handset the type, handfed the hand-cranked press, handfolded the two-up sheet. He sold subscriptions and advertising, staved off creditors..."

Avery L. Kizer may not have known it then, but those were truly fitting words about *Record* founder Irving Martin. In fact, the printer-turned-newspaper publisher was known as a young man with "...a stick of type, a dream and somebody else's money," according to Kizer.

Indeed, Martin's philosophy, competitiveness and unrelentless energy worked. Today, it continues through the efforts of nearly 400 employees which produce *The Record*, Stockton's daily newspaper serving communities throughout San Joaquin and the Mother Lode.

Martin began his dream with the publication of the first *Record*, then known as the *Evening Record*. At the time, competition was fierce for the title of Stockton's daily newspaper, so much so that *The Evening Mail* and *The Morning Independent* did not recognize *The Record*'s existence for nearly two years.

Martin had been determined, first by serving as an apprentice then reporter at *The Independent*, later by acquiring a printing plant that had started a departed rival, *The Republican*.

With a former co-worker, E.H. Fontecilla, at the mechanical helm, Martin began to concentrate his efforts on editorial and advertising. The first issue of *The Stockton Evening Record* was published April 8, 1895 and with it fostered success. After three years, Martin purchased Fontecilla's share of the business.

In the next few years, Martin saw the paper gain little by little in circulation and advertising. By 1905, a $10,000 press was installed, giving *The Record* an edge over the competition.

Five years later, Martin was out of debt, and with a $5,000 accumulated nest egg, he bargained everything to begin building what stands today as *The Record*'s facility on East Market Street.

With the new building came new technology, in the form of a $100,000 press and rows of typesetting machines. Long hours were demanded of Martin and his crew, but Martin was never above socializing nor interacting with members of his *Record* "family."

That sense of family continued at *The Record* until 1952, when Martin turned over his duties as publisher to grandson Irving L. Martin. The elder Martin's son, Irving Martin, Jr., had been vice president of *The Record* corporation at his death in 1944. Martin himself remained chairman of the board until his death in November, 1952.

Like his grandfather and father before him, Irving L. Martin continued the family tradition. Through his 16 years as publisher, the younger Martin oversaw construction of an additional two-story building at

Irving Martin, a printer-turned-publisher who founded the first Record *in 1895.*

Market and American streets and complete reconstruction of the former newspaper plant, including a new Goss Headliner press which allowed the paper to grow from a 64-page capacity to 112 pages.

After Irving L. Martin's death in 1968, his wife served as assistant publisher and vice-president for acting publisher Clyde Long until Jan. 13, 1969, when she sold *The Record* to

Crowd gathered in front of the Record Building to watch progress of the 1925 World Series games between New York Yankees and the New York Giants. The game was transmitted live over the news wire and the scoreboard updated as new information was received.

Speidel Newspapers, Inc. In her last words to *Record* readers the next day, Mrs. Martin expressed her difficult decision.

"When driven by those two great inevitables, death and taxes, to sell the corporate shares in *The Stockton Record,* the Martin heritage therefore was much in mind. It is consistent with that heritage, I believe, that I chose Speidel Newspapers, Inc., a group owned by newspapermen, as the purchaser most likely to preserve the values of a community newspaper. Yet it is with pangs that I am sure are shared with many *Record* readers that tomorrow I will see the name of Martin replaced finally in *The Record's* masthead..."

A new era with Speidel Newspapers at the helm began with *Record* associate publisher Robert B. Whittington named as publisher. Through Whittington's leadership, *The Record* added a Sunday edition to its daily run. The newspaper also celebrated its first 75 years and the addition of an automated typecasting system in 1970. Ironically, "cold type," stories written and edited on video display manuals, did not make its way to *The Record* until 1978, during Robert Uecker's tenure as publisher.

Ownership in *The Record* would change hands once again in 1977 with its acquisition by giant communications company Gannett. Its ownership would oversee several publishers, technology breakthroughs via computers and even open news meetings, offering readers a chance to sit in on the 3:30 p.m. daily sessions.

In 1994, *The Record* was acquired by the Omaha World-Herald Company. Solidifying their commitment to the revitalization of downtown Stockton, over $4 million was invested in building renovations.

The Record continues its leadership role in the community through financial and editorial commitments to non-profit and community service

organizations, including the Business Leadership Summit, the United Way and the relocation of the San Francisco 49ers Training Camp to Stockton. *The Record* has established San Joaquin A+, a grass-roots campaign aimed at increasing local educational achievements through community and business support. Their annual community event aimed at literacy and education, Family Day at the Park, continues to grow in popularity.

Building on its one-hundred-year history, *The Record* looks toward the

Record's editorial department, circa 1940.

future with new, innovative ideas. Web surfers can read local stories at "recordnet.com" and a new alliance with the Tracy Press has brought *The Sunday Record* into Tracy homes. Newspaper circulation has increased by 14.6 percent under the Omaha umbrella while six daily sections bring news, business and sports to 253,900 readers each week.

Record Building, circa 1930-1935.

R.E. SERVICE COMPANY, INC.

R. E. Service Company, Inc. manufactures and distributes a variety of materials used in the production of printed circuit boards, which function as the brain and nerve centers of most consumer and industrial electronic products. Anyone who owns an automobile, stereo, VCR or television very likely have some RES products in their equipment.

Twenty years ago, RES was merely the dream of 19 year-old, Mark Frater, a drill operator who noticed an industry niche that was not being adequately served by his employer's suppliers. With a small loan from his grandmother and the assistance of Robert Ellis (whose initials are part of the RES name) a company was organized.

Lodi warehouse facility.

Like most new businesses, there were many obstacles to overcome. There was insufficient capital, a shortage of qualified personnel and many formidable competitors, to name a few. Frater, relying on his tenacity and business intuition persevered, and by 1981 had the confidence to purchase Ellis' interest in the new company, and to assume the role of president of the newly created corporation, R. E. Services Company, Inc.

Approximately 150 employees work for RES today, most at the Lodi, California manufacturing plant and administrative offices. The RES move to Lodi in 1994 from Sunnyvale, California, was necessary to accommodate its customers' burgeoning demand for RES products which include a variety of drilling support material, metallic foils, tooling plates press pads and films.

Mark Frater retains the position of president and C. E. O. and shares his executive duties with Brian Campbell, the Lodi Plant manager, Daniel Magsaysay, purchasing manager and Mike Mantelle, sales and marketing manager.

During twenty years at the RES helm, Frater has had to make many tough decisions. He believes one of his best was the 1994 decision to purchase the abandoned 100,000 square foot Lodi manufacturing building the company occupies today. He has found the Lodi City officials to be helpful and accommodating in the company's efforts to grow and provide jobs in the community. His goal is to validate their support by doubling RES sales and work force over the next five years.

Like many men who have come up the ladder of success, Frater has not forgotten his roots as a drill operator. He takes satisfaction in improving his employees working conditions and monetary rewards. Last year he established a profit sharing

Aluminum lamination separators.

Lodi manufacturing facility.

retirement plan to which a month's pay is contributed by the company each year on behalf of eligible employees.

The current financial crisis in Asia has created many new challenges for the company and the electronics industry, but Frater is confident that this current crisis, like others, shall also pass. Although the company is already a world leader with some of their products, Frater does not intend to slow down. He plans to add new products, employees and customers to position the company to accommodate what he expects will be the rapidly expanding demands from the electronics industry.

The history of the company already proves that Mark Frater knows how to do that. His vision is unlimited on the threshold of the new millennium in which electronics will continue to be a leading industry.

SIEGFRIED ENGINEERING, INC.

Robert W. Siegfried established Siegfried Engineering, Inc. in Stockton in 1955 as a consulting-engineering firm seeking to do business primarily in Stockton and San Joaquin County. James F. Yost and Arnold R. Schamber soon joined him as partners, and during the years following the Korean War—and extending well into the mid-1960s—the owners and their associates concentrated on becoming an integral factor in the subdivision boom that characterized the explosive growth of Stockton at the time. In overseeing the construction of a series of typical housing developments during those early years, the company consultants gained the experience, expertise and reputation for quality performance that later gained them entry to participate in all steps of the planning, design and construction of much larger planned communities, such as Lincoln Village West, Quail Lakes, and Brookside.

Having expanded the scope of their operations over the intervening decades, Siegfried consultants continue to work closely with architects and developers during site preparation, land use planning, and structural design of a wide array of residential, commercial and industrial projects and with owners during the delicate steps of drawing up contracts and letting bids for construction, equipment installation and other matters. Later in the construction process, they support contractors and subcontractors and in ensuring that original plans come to fruition.

In addition to the creation of planned communities, from the late 1960s into the 1980s, Siegfried Engineering moved into the fields of GPS surveying and construction of upper-scale housing, golf courses, bridges, and a vast array of civil and structural engineering tasks associated with residential, commercial and industrial projects. Its long list of clients grew to include public agencies, land developers, contractors, private owners, and titans of industry, and also with a focus on building activity related to plant construction for the food and

Quail Lakes Planned Community Development, near the I-5 freeway is one of Siegfried Engineering's projects.

wine industry in the San Joaquin Valley.

As time passed, the original owners retired. Having tenures with the company dating as far back as the 1960s, the current owners are Wayne M. West, president; Lex A. Corrales, vice president, Steve R. Thumlert, vice president, and Anthony J. Lopes, secretary, treasurer and vice president. Still centering their attention on Stockton and San Joaquin County, with ventures into the Central Valley and the Bay Area when

tempting prospects arise, the Siegfried partners take pride in performing the key industrial site engineering and construction consultation involved in the erection of numerous landmarks that dot the region—notably but far from limited to: Nestle Distribution Facility-Lathrup, CA; Brookside Country Club championship golf course; FEMA flood protection levees for Stockton; Brookside Estates, Quail Lakes and Lincoln Village West planned community developments, Stockton; Greenhaven Subdivision, Sacramento; Weberstown Mall, Stockton; Kirkwood Meadows Ski Resort; Johnson Wax Building, Woodland; U.S. Sprint Company relay facility, Stockton; Dana Corporation-Toyota Truck Frame Assembly Plant, Stockton, and Stockton Channel seawall.

With 32 employees working out of their offices at 4045 Coronado Avenue in Stockton, the Siegfried owners look forward to the pleasant business of continuing to please a long-established clientele and looking forward to an equal slate of satisfied new customers.

Siegfried Engineering's project pictured here is Children's home of Stockton.

STOCKTON TERMINAL AND EASTERN RAILROAD

"Not as long but just as wide." Stockton's own railroad lives up to its motto. The Stockton Terminal and Eastern Railroad spreads wide in East Stockton.

The president of the railroad, Thomas K. Beard purchased the line, known locally as the Slow Tired & Easy Railroad in 1958. Under his leadership the company has built and controls three million square feet of warehouses. Fairchild Industrial Park was developed and is serviced by the S. T. & E. which connects with the Burlington Northern-Santa Fe and the Union Pacific Railroad, the only two rail lines that service the West Coast today. The company has 200 cars of rolling stock. The current corporation officers serving under Beard's leadership are: Greg Carney, vice president and chief operating officer, Robert Jenkins, vice president, Diane Musto. secretary/treaurer.

The S. T. & E. Railroad was organized as a corporation in 1908. By September of 1910 the rails had been laid to Linden, east of Stockton, so the

Today's main terminal building and railhead.

little town put on a big celebration. The railroad's original destination was Jenny Lind in Calaveras County, however it was never completed beyond Belotta. The railroad went through economic ups and downs with a succession of presidents and operations managers. Joe Dietrich, a Stockton Realtor, managed the road from 1917 until 1952.

A Los Angeles Chiropodist, Dr. John Hiss, who was a real railroad buff purchased the road. It appeared he purchased it so he could operate a locomotive, but he lost interest by 1958. This was when "Tom" Beard from the Beard railroad family in Modesto, purchased the S. T. & E. Railroad. One of his motives was to provide an activity for his 65 year old father, George Beard. George Beard was a second generation railroader and past president of the Modesto Empire and Traction Company in Modesto. Tom worked on the railroad in Modesto when he was a teenager. After college he enlisted in the Army and was picked to serve in the first Army Transportation Corps organized during W W II. He was in charge of

transportation of all perishable goods in Europe during the Allied Invasion and under the Marshall Plan following the war. He finally returned to the Modesto railroad.

The Beards vowed they would change the name of their new S. T. & E. Railroad to "Strong, Tenacious and Energetic." After his father died, Tom put his energy into the road and the development of industrial warehouses on the line in East Stockton. He secured the status of a Terminal Railroad which gave the company a better share of rates and the business flourished.

Beard serves on the Board of Directors of the State Railroad Museum in Sacramento. He donated steam Locomotive #3 to the Museum. As this book goes to press he is making plans to donate antique parlor and passengers cars to the Golden Gate Railway Museum at China Basin in San Francisco.

For a complete history of the S. T. & E. Railroad, see the book "The Slow Tired and Easy Railroad," by Olive Davis published in 1976 by Valley Publishers.

ST. JOSEPH'S MEDICAL CENTER

St. Joseph's Home and Hospital was founded a century ago by Reverend William B. O'Connor. In 1898, Stockton founder, Captain Charles M. Weber donated five acres of land to Fr. O'Connor, the pastor of St Mary's Parish, as a home for older men. Several leading doctors joined Fr. O'Connor in realizing the need for a hospital to serve not only the growing city of Stockton, but the surrounding districts in the San Joaquin Valley. On March 19, 1899, the corner-stone was laid by the Archbishop of San Francisco, the Most Reverend Patrick W. Riordan.

St. Joseph's formally opened on December 21, 1899 with 25 hospital beds. Fr. O'Connor invited the Dominican Sisters of San Rafael, who were teaching in local schools, to staff the hospital and home. Upon his death in 1911, Fr. O'Connor transferred ownership and operation of the hospital to the Dominican Sisters.

Shortly after the opening of the Hospital, the Sisters felt that a Nurse's Training School was necessary. In 1902, St. Joseph's opened the area's first school of Nursing for the purpose of training nurses for the community.

Reverend William B. O'Connor, 1841-1911, founder of St. Joseph's Home and Hospital.

St. Joseph's Home and Hospital opened its doors to the Stockton community on December 21, 1899.

Because of Stockton's growing population, St. Joseph's added 100 beds in 1916. In the early 1920s, St. Joseph's added what at that time was considered the most modern x-ray equipment in the area. Through the degree of excellence being provided at St. Joseph's, the hospital received in these early days the first of its continuing certificates of accreditation from the American College of Surgeons.

During the difficult years of the depression, St. Joseph's remained open and responsive to the growing medical needs of the community. The troubled years of World War II saw the community and hospital depleted of services and personnel necessary to everyday existence; nonetheless, St. Joseph's worked to provide to the community the best health care possible.

Nineteen forty-eight saw the opening of the Rheumatic Fever Ward, under the sponsorship of the Junior Aid of Stockton, for the care of children. The next major addition took place in 1954 to include the addition of 54 beds.

As the population of Stockton grew in the early 1960s, the hospital continued to respond by adding additional beds and services to meet the demands of the community. Several departments were moved to a larger addition which would house Surgery Suites, Recovery Room, Intensive Care Unit, Pediatrics, Radiology, Laboratory, Emergency, Medical Records, Admitting and Business Office. Another 90 beds were added to the Hospital during this time.

In 1974, doctors performed the first open heart surgery for the area at St. Joseph's. In March 1996, St. Joseph's Heart Center opened to provide its cardiac program with highly skilled physicians; the latest in technology and dedicated and experienced professional patient care staff.

A leader in health care today, St. Joseph's Medical Center is a not-for-profit, acute care community hospital specializing in heart, cancer, respiratory and emergency services.

As St. Joseph's approaches its 100 year Centennial, the dream of the founders lives on today through the commitment to its mission; to continuously improve the health and well-being of its communities.

SELECTED BIBLIOGRAPHY

Allen, Glen, and Young, Chas. H. *Architecture.* Stockton, Ca.: Monograph, 1929.

Bailey, Edgar H. *"Geology of Northern California."* San Francisco: Bulletin 190, U.S. Geological Survey (1966), California Div. of Mines.

Bancroft, Hubert Howe. *California Pioneer Register.* Baltimore: Regional Publishing, 1964.

Barrett, S.A., and Gifford, E.W. *Miwok Natural Culture.* Yosemite National Park, Ca.: Yosemite Natural History Association, 1959.

Bennyhoff, James Allen. *Ethnogeography of the Plains Miwok.* Davis, Ca.: University of California at Davis, 1977.

Bryant, Edwin. *What I Saw In California.* Santa Ana, Ca.: The Fine Arts Press, 1936.

Cook, Sherburne F. *"The Aboriginal Population of the San Joaquin Valley California,"* Berkeley and Los Angeles, Ca.: Anthropological Records, Vol. 16 (No. 2), University of California Press, Berkeley, 1955.

_____ . *"Expeditions to the Interior of California's Central Valley from 1820-1840."* Berkeley and Los Angeles, Ca.: Vol. 20 (No. 5), Anthropological Records. University of California Press, 1962.

Derbec, Etienne. *A French Journalist in California.* Georgetown, Ca.: Edited by A.P. Nasatire. Talisman Press, 1964.

Dillion, Richard. *Fool's Gold: Captain John Sutter.* Santa Cruz, CA.: Western Tanager, 1967.

Duran, Narcisco. *Diary of Fray Narcisco Duran: Expedition on the Sacramento and San Joaquin Rivers in 1817.* Berkeley, Ca.: University of California, 1911.

Gilbert, F.T. *History of San Joaquin County.* Oakland, Ca.: Thompson & West, 1879.

Grunsky, Carl Ewald. *Stockton Boyhood.* Berkeley, Ca.: Friends of the Bancroft Library, 1959.

Gunter, Elder. *The City of Stockton: Past, Present & Future.* Stockton, Ca.: Private Printing, 1977.

Hammond, George, and Morgan, Dale. *Captain Charles M. Weber.* Berkeley, Ca.: The Friends of the Bancroft Library, 1966.

Hartmann, Ilka. *The Youth Charles M. Weber, Founder of Stockton.* Stockton, Ca.: University of the Pacific, 1979.

Hollembeak, J.R. *A History of the Public Schools of Stockton California.* Stockton, Ca.: Private Printing, 1909.

Hutchinson, W.H. *California, The Golden Shore by the Sundown Sea.* Palo Alto, Ca. Star Publishing, 1980.

Johnson, Herbert B. *Discrimination Against the Japanese in California.* Berkeley, Ca.: R&E Research Association, 1971.

Kennedy, Glen. *It Happened in Stockton.* Stockton, Ca.: Private Printing, 1967.

Kroeber, A.L. *Handbook of the Indians of California.* Berkeley, Ca.: California Book Company, 1952.

_____ . *"Yokuts Dialect Survey."* Berkeley, Ca.: Anthropological Records, Vol. 11 (No. 3), University of California Press, 1961.

Latta, F.F. *Handbook of Yokuts Indians.* Bakersfield, Ca.: Kern County Museum, 1949.

Lyman, George D. *John Marsh, Pioneer.* New York: Charles Scribners Sons, 1930.

Maloney, Alice Bay. *Fur Brigade to the Bonaventura: John Works California Expedition 1832-1833.* San Francisco, Ca.: California Historical Society, 1945.

Margolin, Malcolm. *The Ohlone Way.* Berkeley, Ca.: Heyday Books, 1978.

_____ . *The Way We Lived.* Berkeley, Ca.: Heyday Books, 1981.

McAfee, Ward. *California Railroad Era, 1850-1911.* San Marino, Ca.: Golden West Books, 1973.

McComb, Delmar M., Jr. *The City of Great Peace.* Stockton, Ca.: Private Printing, 1961.

_____ . *Beat! Beat! Drums!, A History of Stockton During the Civil War.* Stockton, Ca.: Private Printing, 1965.

Miller, William J. *California Through the Ages.* Los Angeles, Ca.: Westernlore Press, 1957.

Minnick, Sylvia Sun. *Chinese in San Joaquin County.* Sacramento, Ca.: Thesis, Sacramento State University, 1983.

Norris, Robert Matheson, and Webb, Robert W. *Geology of California.* New York: Wiley, 1976.

Oakeshott, Gordon B. *California's Changing Landscape.* New York: McGraw Hill, 1978.

Pellegrini, Albert. *Stockton's Reaction to Europe and Mexican Involvement 1914-1918.* Stockton, Ca.: Thesis, San Joaquin Delta College History 10, 1973.

Penrose, Eldon R. *California Nativism: Organized Opposition to Japanese, 1890-1913.* San Francisco: Reprint, R&E Research Association, 1973.

Ragir, Sonia. *The Early Horizon in Central California Prehistory.* Berkeley, Ca.: University of California, Department of Anthropology, 1972.

Roberts, James Arthur. *Stockton Manufacturing.* San Jose, Ca.: Smith & McKay Printing, 1978.

Taylor, Bayard. *Eldorado or Adventure in the Path of an Empire.* New York: G.P. Putnam, 1868.

Taylor, Clotilde Grunsky. *Dear Family.* Stockton, Ca.: Private Printing, 1929.

Tinkham, George H. *History of San Joaquin County, California.* Los Angeles: Historic Record Company, 1923.

Winther, Ocsar O. *Express and Stagecoach Days in California.* Palo Alto, Ca.: Stanford University Press, 1936.

_____ . Works Progress Administration of the City of Stockton. *History of San Joaquin County.* Stockton, Ca.: Private Printing, 1938.

INDEX